Small Mercies

For Cary,
with a lot of love,
respect + fellow Yankeeism.

Barbara

Greedy for the small mercies of this world,
they remain blind to the great suffering to come.

—Bodhidharma

Small Mercies

BARBARA McCAULEY

SHERMAN
ASHER
Publishing

ACKNOWLEDGMENTS
   Cover Art : Alvaro Cardona-Hine "Flowers for the Beloved"
   Title Page : sketch by Barbara McCauley
   Cover Design : Janice St. Marie
   Book Design : Judith Rafaela
   Printed in the United States of America

ISBN (hardcover) 1-890932-04-03
(trade paper) 1-890932-05-1

First Edition

      Library of Congress Cataloging-in-Publication Data

McCauley, Barbara, 1939–
      Small mercies / Barbara McCauley. --1st ed.
         p.   cm.
      ISBN 1-890932-04-3 (alk. paper)
         1.Suicide--United States--Psychological aspects. 2. Suicide
   victims--United States--Family relationships. 3. Bereavement-
   United States.   I. Title.
      HV6548.U5M33   1998
      362.28'3'093--dc21   98-29013
                                                       CIP

                  Sherman Asher Publishing
                        PO Box 2853
                      Santa Fe, NM 87504
               Changing the World One Book at a Time ™

for my sister,

brother,

and for

Karen, Scott,

Kelly and David

AUTHOR'S NOTE

The material in this book is organized in alternating sections of longer memories of events and shorter reflections on the facts of my sister's death. I wanted the memories to be informed with the fact of her death as they are in my life so that you, the reader, could travel with me as I recreate the small mercies that give so much apparent consolation. These memories sections are arranged chronologically from childhood to young womanhood and head, so to speak, toward Lisa's death. The reflections start after that fact and move backwards in time to about a year before she killed herself.

There were six of us in our family: Mother, Dad, Ellie, Lisa, Tommy and I . Ellie was the first-born; two years later came Lisa; two years later again, Tommy; one year later, me, the last.

For reasons of privacy I have changed the names of some people.

INTRODUCTION

When Lisa died, I took off the three days allotted by my employer for grief. I believed death could be absorbed, that it would sink inside me the way an object sinks in water. Others had survived. And my employer allowed three days, an apparently agreed-upon number sufficient for everyone. I would get over it. What did I know? I was young. I knew little about the biology of grief; nothing of its profound intimacy. And Lisa did not simply die. She killed herself. She was my sister, three years older, just thirty.

Over twenty five years have passed since then, and her death has indeed sunk, as I'd expected, deep inside me. But it is, like any underwater object, crusted over with barnacles of guilt, fuzzy with incomprehension and anger. Suicide is not just death. It is an act that insists; it becomes the unanswered questions, the missed opportunities. It doesn't matter what stories I tell myself: I still believe I should have saved her, could have, and didn't. I missed by moments. Now she is my personal ghost whose hauntings get rarer as the years pass, but who returns nevertheless, to remind me that I will never understand, that I will always be responsible.

When we try to comfort others, most of us choose our words carefully, believing it's what we say: the wisdom, the insight, that consoles. In my experience, this is not true. Grief occurs in the body as much as in the mind. Every cell is heavy with it, and neither words nor ideas relieve that weight. If anything comforts, it is the sounds themselves, the murmurings, the rhythms, the lilt of language so familiar it penetrates.

Over these years, I have used words again and again in various forms—trying to find understanding is what I thought— when, in fact, the words have been a song to myself, a kind of self-embrace, a motherly rocking and holding. And I've struggled to bring this material into some kind of synthesis—suicide does not lend itself to perfect understanding, nor to completion—but the hidden difficulty was that I was still holding a grudge: Lisa hurt me, she had no right. In the last year (1992) when I finally pushed to finish this as a book, I began to see Lisa again, I mean to visually remember her, something I had been unable to do since her death. She appeared in dreams, I felt her presence in me. Not ghost-like, or mediumistically, nothing like that. More as if I'd finally walked into the room within myself where I'd put her away. She had so many stories to tell me.

The events here happened to me and my family. The only way I can talk about Lisa is to write of my own experience, and my sense of our family life. So these are my truths. To write of Lisa as if I knew her and was intimate with her experience would be to create fiction. Memory is fiction enough, that realm in which we create our own life stories. Objective reality is not so solid an affair as most of us would like to believe.

So this is not a book about understanding. Nor is it about justification. Neither are possible. Only compassion and forgiveness can penetrate the perplexing reality of a young woman choosing to kill herself; they are what we need to heal from what is a brutal wound. And they come in their own way, in their own time. They cannot be forced.

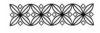

Lisa was the story-teller; my brother, Tommy, and I were her audience. Where my father would sit down with an Aesop's fable or a tale from *The Thousand and One Nights*, Lisa would simply look off into the distance and begin. Stories spilled out of her with such ease that there seemed to be nothing special to it; thus my amazement when I would try to imitate her gift and nothing would emerge other than that magical first line followed by profound puzzlement. Where did they come from in her? *Once upon a time*, she would say, and Tommy and I would settle down to enter the world she revealed to us in her words. She made everything seem possible, so that the day she announced the fairy queen was about to appear in the orchard next door and that I could talk to her, I was only mildly skeptical.

"How do you know she'll come?"

"Oh, I know," Lisa answered. "You'd better get ready."

That was enough. Lisa was very serious. She had told me about fairies, and showed me where in the violet patch down in the woods she had once seen one. "Tiny," she had said, "no bigger than your thumb. And bright."

"Well? Get ready," she repeated.

"How do I do that?"

She sighed heavily. "I've told you that before."

I remembered. Lisa had said that fairies could only be seen by the pure ones, the pure ones being those without sin. And since I had not yet made my First Communion, she had taught me another way to get rid of my sins.

"It works just as good," she had said. Even then, so young, she had a deep, somewhat husky voice, with an inevitable stoppage in her throat which she constantly cleared.

I went to the slope behind our house and sat on the grass. "You throw your sins, one by one, up onto the passing clouds and let them sail away." When I asked what would happen when the clouds got full of sins, she smiled wisely. "No, that's why it rains. When the clouds get full of sins, they turn dark and drop them down in the rain." She shrugged. "Then they get clean and white again."

This day of the fairy queen's appearance was a good one for throwing away sins. Large white clouds drifted high in the sky.

"I was late for dinner," I whispered, and willed my lateness onto the soft curve of a huge cloud. It drifted to my right. "And I disobeyed three times."

I chose three separate clouds, counting out the three occurences as I flung them, one after another, up into the sky. I couldn't think of anything else then, and sat up. At seven, sins were hard to come by.

The orchard was to my right, but the big forsythia bush blocked any view of it. Lisa's voice reached me from beyond the forsythia.

"Are you ready yet?" I called out.

She did not answer, and I was tempted to get up and peek when she appeared around the side of the bush.

"You have to be quiet. She doesn't just come easy." Lisa warned, "And if you peek, she won't come at all."

I wondered if I should consider my temptation to peek a sin and give it to the clouds when she whispered, "Psst, come on."

She waved her chubby arm as a signal to follow. Was it really going to happen? I was sure I couldn't be easily fooled. I got up and walked with her around the bush.

"Where?" I asked.

Lisa pointed solemnly to the smallest apple tree that stood second in a row of four on the woods side of the orchard. There I saw a tiny figure in pink and white standing at the base of the tree in a patch of sunlight. Lisa beamed at me.

"Come on," she said quietly. "She'll talk to you."

I could not take my eyes off the small creature under the tree. I was reminded of the fancy dolls kept on the highest shelf at Crook's drug store, dolls my mother said were useless and too expensive, that looked out from their boxes, one arm raised against the wide circle of a satin dress. This small figure was that size and wore a white gown with a pink band around her waist. She did not move until I sat down in the spot Lisa pointed out to me a few feet in front of the fairy queen. Then she flew up, her whole body rising with a jerk like a hummingbird. One arm rose as if in greeting. A small voice, high and sweet, greeted me.

"Hi. Are you Barbara?"

She was real!

I watched as the little queen lowered herself and a few silver flecks of dust dropped from her hair catching the sun like shooting stars and disappearing into the long, green grass. I scarcely heard the queen's words as she raised and lowered her arms and flew up and down.

"Do you believe in fairies now?" the queen asked.

"Oh yes, yes I do."

"Remember. You must always be a good girl and obey your parents."

"Yes I will. Thank you, fairy queen."

I sensed it was over already and quickly asked, "Will you come back? Can I see you again?"

The queen's laugh was like tiny bells. I thought I saw her smiling as she flew up and turned pirouettes.

"Yes, I will come to see you again," her little voice said and she flew up high into the leaves of the apple tree and was gone. Lisa shook me by the shoulder and said I had to leave now, that whatever I did, I must not turn around to look at the tree, or come back here until she said I could.

"Why?" I needed to have reasons for things.

Lisa answered solemnly. "Because if you turn around to peek, or if you come back, you will never see the fairy queen again."

I was careful to keep my eyes straight ahead as I walked in a direct line from the tree toward the street in front of our house. I would not even look up or down for fear my eyes might betray me and swing to the side before I realized it. The long grasses tangled around my feet and ankles, almost tripping me until I reached the clipped lawn at the edge of the orchard. Even then, I almost turned without thinking.

I sat at the edge of the lawn that lay like a shore at the dead end of the road, the black tar rippled up against it in small waves. The length of my back felt as if it had opened up and a wholly different set of sensors picked up the slightest movements and sounds behind me. There were soft bursts of giggles and, with a thrill, I supposed the fairy queen was still nearby, perhaps in the company of lesser fairies.

A movement to my right, just on the periphery of my vision, made my eyes swing involuntarily to take it in and, before I had time to realize, I saw Margie, the girl from next door, walking fast behind the back hedge toward her own house, a box held tightly in front of her. And in the same flash, I glimpsed also the small apple tree. Lisa was beneath its branches, kneeling in the grass. A surge of horror rose upward from my stomach. I had looked. I had seen the tree.

I bit the feeling back down and my stomach felt queasy from it. A small piece of glass was embedded, as it had been for months now, under the skin of my right knee. I picked at it idly. Lisa had made it perfectly clear: if I looked, I would never see the fairy queen again. I would have liked to hope that because no one, except myself, knew what I had done, that it would not count against me. But the feeling in my body told me it was already done, that it did not matter whether anyone else knew or not, because I did, and if I knew, then certainly the fairy queen, like God, would know.

Footsteps came through the grass behind me and Lisa appeared at my side, out of breath. She was beaming, her pretty face flushed with the heat of the summer afternoon. I considered telling her what had happened. Lisa would know how to make it all right if that was possible.

"Did you look?" she demanded, standing above me, her hands on her hips.

The *no* slipped out before I had a chance to stop it. Lisa looked searchingly at me.

"Are you sure?"

I was a poor liar. Somehow the truth leaked out somewhere in my face, so I forced myself to believe in the lie, to hold Lisa's eyes as I repeated it.

"No, I didn't look. Why would I look?"

She gazed off down the street, then sat beside me. Her eyes were bright and happy.

"So what do you think?"

I was enmeshed in my guilt, the magic of the moments under the tree already spoiled. "Huh?" I asked.

"Stupid. What do you think of the queen?"

The magic returned a moment. I lit up under its spell. "Oh, she's beautiful! Gosh, Lisa, how did you get her to come?"

"That's my secret. Someday maybe you'll be able to do it too."

"After I make my First Communion?"

Lisa looked puzzled. "What's that got to do with it?"

"I don't know. I just thought...." I did not know what I thought.

"Sometimes you're so dumb," she said. She rose.

"When can I see her again? Will she come back?"

"Oh, we'll see. Maybe she'll come back tomorrow." Lisa was getting ready to leave. "I wonder where Margie is."

"She's home. I saw her going there a few minutes ago."

Lisa turned upon me. "Then you looked! You turned around!"

"No, I didn't! I just saw Margie go past the hedge. She...she was carrying something."

Lisa pursed her lips the way Mother did when she was angry. "Liar! If you looked...."

"I didn't, I tell you! I didn't!" I could not look at her. The mistake overwhelmed me. Yet, oddly, when Lisa demanded I say it again, looking her in the eye as I said it, a transformation took place. I stood up and faced her squarely.

With a sense of great dignity and control, I said, "I did not look. So there." With that, I stomped off across the front lawn to the house, climbed the steps and slammed the screen door behind me. I hated to be called a liar, regardless of its accuracy.

The incident was forgotten by dinnertime and neither Lisa nor I mentioned the fairy queen at all. At bedtime, she came into the room I shared with my brother and whispered, "She's coming tomorrow. In the morning."

In the darkness I turned from side to side, alternating between the desire to see the fairy queen again, my wonder at her presence, at the incredible brightness of the light that fell on her or emanated from her, and the anxiety that I had spoiled everything. But, if the fairy queen had already agreed to come, then perhaps she did not know, or she understood that it was an accident for which I was not responsible. I had seen nothing unusual, only the tree as it always was and Lisa kneeling in the grass. It was a long time before I fell asleep.

In the morning I ran outside to the embankment. The day was overcast, no single sin-catching cloud in sight. I closed my eyes tight and willed up both my accident and my lies hoping my sins would find a corner to cling to in the mass of grey. I lay back on the grass, allowing its cool dampness to soak into my shorts and top.

Lisa joined me and said that the fairy queen did not like grey days, that she might not come.

"Oh, she's got to come. She's got to."

"Well, we'll see," Lisa said. "Wait here. I'll see what I can do." She got up and went toward Margie's house next door.

"Will it be soon?" I called out after her.

"Stay there. I'll be right back."

Margie's back screen door snapped shut a few minutes later and I expected Lisa to appear around the corner of the garage. When she did not, I got up and ran to Margie's house.

Margie's mother came to the door.

"Is my sister here?"

"Nope. They just went out."

I turned away. It would not happen then. Not if Lisa went somewhere with Margie. I returned to the embankment and lay back down to recall yet another time the deliciousness of the previous day. Until then, I had almost not believed fairies existed. But I saw the queen fly right in front of me, I heard her small high voice with my own ears. I believed in God with far less to go on. Overnight I had been able to convince myself that if God forgave the evil in me, then certainly the fairy queen should make allowances for accidents. So when Lisa returned a short time later to announce that the queen was waiting in the orchard to see me, I jumped up.

"Did you have any trouble getting her?" I asked.

"Oh no. I can get her to come anytime I want to. But she likes sunny days better."

"Sure, me too."

The two of us walked through the grass to the tree. In the distance, the fairy queen looked even tinier than yesterday. No bright patch of light surrounded her today.

I squatted in the same place as before and looked at the queen. She looked different: duller, stiffer. But suddenly, she flew straight up in the air about halfway between the ground and the low first branch of the apple tree.

"Hi Barbara," she said, bobbing up and down. "How are you today?"

"Oh fine," I answered and wondered at the loss of something I already felt rising inside me. It rose the way crying did, inside my throat.

"Did you look yesterday?" the queen asked. She dropped down to the grass. The area where she stood was flattened, the grass tamped down.

I was stunned. The queen repeated the question. Impatience was in her voice.

"I...I didn't," I said finally. As I said it, the queen rose and suddenly stopped short as though stuck, her body rotating from side to side. She looked dead hanging there like that. Then I saw the fishing lines. They were tied almost invisibly around each of the queen's tiny wrists and around her waist. They rose up, looped over the branches of the tree and down again behind the tree trunk.

"You have to go now, fast!" Lisa insisted, pulling me around. "The queen's sick or something. You have to *go!*"

I pulled free from Lisa's grip and stared at the fairy queen.

"She's not real," I said. "You tricked me."

Lisa pulled my arm.

"No, she's real. Don't look at her now. Something's wrong." There was pleading in Lisa's voice.

I met her eyes. In that moment I saw my own loss reflected there. Then the tears just at the edge of Lisa's eyes spilled out into a sudden recognition.

"Oh! I know what happened! I know!" Lisa cried out. "You looked yesterday, didn't you?"

So this was what happened. This was what the nuns meant by evil. And while I certainly understood that Lisa and Margie, whose head peered out now from behind the trunk of the tree, had really tricked me, I also understood that I was somehow responsible for this turn of events, that I too participated in the transformation of what had been real and magic yesterday into this present fake—a doll with strings, a mere puppet dangling from the tree limb. Lisa was right: I had ruined everything by looking.

I jumped up and began running through the grass toward the house. I wanted to escape; I wanted to run from this loss. Lisa's voice would not let me.

"You looked," she kept crying out. The words became a rasping chant. "You looked! You looked!"

What's left, afterwards. A closet filled with clothes that finally go to cousins since neither my sister Ellie nor I could bear to wear them. Drawers and cabinets of kitchen utensils, linens, china, everything necessary for future evenings of entertaining at home. Furniture, jewelry, shoes, chests filled with underwear, papers, photographs. All of it belonging to no one. A reverse robbery.

A distraught landlord: *She could have blown up the whole building.* Not upset so much at that really, as at her doing this to him. He has every right to take it personally. The smell of gas finally seeped out through the towel she'd placed along the bottom of the door, and there she was, in her robe on the sofa, the half-drunk glass of wine, the emptied bottle of pills on the table beside her.

My brother gets the job of taking care of all this: the identification, the disposal, the notification. Did he go to the morgue? I've never asked. I have always imagined that he went there, to her apartment, and said, *Yes, that is my sister,* looking right at her. Which is why I have never asked. This was the last moment in her life, the last thing to connect her to us, when Tommy stood ten feet away and looked at her, his eyes brimming the way no stranger's would.

Later I received a box, no bigger than a shipment of books, containing some of her possessions. I'd known they were coming so I was prepared to receive something, though I didn't know what. What I was not prepared for was the size of that box, her life's possessions pared down to so small a container; and that not one of the objects gave me anything of her. Even the tiny silver spoons she'd received as a gift when we were both in Finland signified nothing.

Without me to recognize them, they were anybody's spoons, simple everyday objects one might find under glass in a thrift store.

I still have these remnants of Lisa's life. I still cherish them, and I remember her each time I dust or use one of them. But I've learned that we cannot count on objects. They hang on to nothing, not our love or our memories. They showed me just how quickly we disappear.

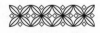

My friend Maria was as pretty as her mother, with the same wide open face, large brown eyes, and upturned nose. But where Mrs. Papetto was only somewhat simple in her ways, in her uncreased forehead that mirrored her freedom from worry or thought, Maria was devoid of any ability to associate one thing with another in any halfway intelligent way. Two years from this day when we played in her room, she would announce to me that she could sit on a phonograph record without breaking it. She would pick my favorite polka, a 78, old, and brittle.

"No," I would cry, "not that one!"

"But I'm not going to break it. Let me show you."

I grabbed her arm, but she finally convinced me; she'd seen it done at her uncle's house; she'd practiced with lots of records and never broken one. I would have felt happier if she'd chosen a record I didn't like, but she insisted it be this one precisely because it was my favorite and she wanted to show me how sure she was. I didn't want to hurt her feelings; besides, I now trusted her.

"Okay. Sit on it."

We were in our basement with its newly-whitewashed walls where my parents had moved the phonograph so Ellie and Lisa could visit with their friends in the only part of the house where they might have a little privacy. There was a hard slat wooden bench and a couple of canvas beach chairs. Maria placed the record gently on a sling-type beach chair and sat down. There was a series of sickening cracks as she sank deeper into the chair.

"Oh, sure. Great, real great, Maria. Oh boy!" I was ready to kill her. "Oh wow, real smart."

She stood up and looked dumbly at the record. "It broke," she said with actual amazement in her voice.

"Oh no, it didn't break. Geez, you're so smart."

She turned to me almost in tears. "But it worked. Let me show you. Let me try another."

"Oh sure. Go through all our records. Sure. You only already broke my favorite one."

She had another record in her hands.

"No!" I screamed. "That's Lisa's."

But she sank down on that one too.

It was too much. "You'd better leave, Maria," I said. "Just go home, please. Now."

To make it worse, Lisa held me responsible. "She's your stupid friend," she said, and wouldn't speak to me for almost a week.

Back in first grade when I'd already caught up with Maria—this was the first time she got held back—I would pass her in the fourth grade when they held her back again—we were rehearsing for our school play. Maria had a part in which she was supposed to hold up a big card with the letter A on it and say: *A is for apple. I am an apple.* Maria had been given the A because she was the tallest.

Maria held up her card on cue.

"A is for apple. I am a apple," she intoned.

Mrs. Judge tapped with her conductor's baton.

"Maria," she called out. Maria fixed her large brown eyes on Mrs. Judge. In the environment of school, nothing could be more vacant than Maria's large brown eyes. "I am *an* apple," Mrs. Judge corrected gently.

Maria just looked at her.

"Now say it, dear. I am *an* apple."

"A is for apple. I am a apple."

A few kids near Maria encouraged her with pokes and whispers. "*An* apple, stupid. Say *an*."

Mrs. Judge repeated. "I am *an* apple."

"I am *a* apple," Maria chimed. Mrs. Judge's face was set firmly into the correction she wanted; there was also a look of profound bewilderment in her eyes.

"*An* apple, dear. Say *an* apple."

"*A* apple."

"Dorie, you change with Maria. Maria, you say, 'B is for ball. I am a ball.'"

Now in the 4th grade for the second time, she still said *a* apple, *a* ice cream. The determiner *an* remained a phonetic mountain she would never climb.

Maria was also a great liar, lied every chance she got, and you could always tell she was lying because it was the only time her eyes showed a glimmer of something like intelligence. Her greatness consisted in quantity alone however, most of her lies so blatant even her mother saw them for what they were. Whenever she did anything wrong, she left a trail a mile wide behind her.

So I was justifiably concerned when Mrs. Papetto called up to us that she was going to the store for bread and, as soon as the front door slammed shut, Maria jumped up with a "Come on," and ran into her parents' bedroom.

"What are you doing?" She was rummaging through the bottom drawer of the dresser.

Maria just rolled her eyes with the promise of something special.

"What if she comes back?" She was bound to get caught. I saw already how she left the contents of the drawer in total disorder. I wasn't sure I wanted to be part of this.

"Look if you want," she said airily. "She's gone."

Mrs. Papetto was just turning onto School St., already a half block away.

"Here it is." She held up what looked like a miniature comic book. "Look at this."

It was March, one of those cold, motionless, grey days, full of a late winter silence. The house around us was even quieter. On the narrow night stand next to the bed, the electric clock buzzed. Downstairs the refrigerator turned off.

I knelt beside her on the floor. Maria moved closer rather than give up possession of the little book. She held it out in front of me.

I was two years younger than Maria, always careful to act as though I were more knowledgeable than my ten years allowed.

But what I beheld on the cover of this little book knocked the pretense out of me. I gasped.

She giggled in response. "It's what men and women do," she said.

I pointed. "What's that?"

"It's the man's thing."

"Oh, come on," I said, in an attempt to recover a more mature stature as well as deny the existence of what I saw. "I've seen my brother's and Billy's and Mike Carmichael's, and they're nothing like that." I shook my head slowly with the weight of my experience.

Maria peered at me. "When?" she challenged.

"Oh, once down the woods. They had a contest to see who could pee the farthest. They made me stand in back of them, but I saw anyway. Not one of them had one bigger than my thumb."

"Well, it's true anyway," Maria asserted.

I did not believe her, but felt acutely uncomfortable with what I recognized in the drawings. Whoever had drawn them had touched on that sense of shame I had grown to associate with what my mother eloquently termed "down there." "Down there" was never spoken of under most circumstances, and it was only with obvious distaste that my mother used the word "crotch", a necessary term when buying me new jeans. *Are they too tight in the crotch?* And we would both blush. But here were the "down theres" and "crotches" below faces that were twisted into large, unnatural grins; whose eyes bulged out of their sockets. I understood their looks, which I misjudged to be shame, what I'd learned from the expression on my mother's face when she caught my cousin and me playing doctor when we were four or five years old. That thrill of sexual pleasure was early associated with a shame so profound it would send blood rushing to my face all the way into my adult years.

"I don't want to see anymore," I said.

"Oh, come on," she pleaded. "Look." She flipped the pages back to the beginning. "It's fun."

"I have to go home." I left over her protests. "Don't tell anyone," she called out after me. "If you do, you're gonna get it!"

Our houses were separated by several open fields. The snow had melted in an earlier thaw, but the earth had stiffened again with the return of the cold. Ice patches, like spider webs, spanned last summer's leftover furrows. I broke every one I came across, intent upon the delicate give, like a fine pane of glass, beneath my shoes. I especially liked the thin mesh of cracks that exploded across the surface just before my foot broke through; and the tinny sound that accompanied the breaking. I breathed in the frigid air, watched my breath leave like the smoke from a small fire, bared my teeth to let the cold hurt them, felt the cold burning to the bottom of my lungs. I wanted to erase everything I'd seen in the book.

But the next time Mrs. Papetto left us alone, Maria did not have to cajole me. This time, there were two books.

"They're my father's," she said.

I was afraid of fathers. They were inaccessible, unpredictable, the ones whose anger counted. Every day they left in their cars to go to remote jobs, and their influence was not felt until they returned in the evening when a more disciplined atmosphere asserted itself. We ate on plates then instead of paper napkins, and the radio droned the news throughout the meal while my father's eyes moved from plate to plate to see that we ate all of our dinner.

But Maria's father embodied something more than this usual dread other fathers inspired. He had a look about him, in the looseness of his lips, which hung slightly open showing the moist underlip, and in the dreaminess of his eyes that regarded you directly but seemed not to see; or would see, for a moment, then transform you into the dream inside his eyes so that you felt absorbed. So of course these books were his. They sprang out of those eyes, out of his careless way of dressing, the baggy grey pants he wore, the shirt that invariably was half-opened, exposing his white T-shirt and a patch of dark hair on his barrel chest.

This time I inspected the books very carefully. As in all comics, there were the usual white clouds filled with dialogue, but I didn't read; I looked. There were no words for what I saw. I had no vocabulary for sexual organs or sexual function, let alone any meaningful framework in which I could place this experience. I decided I would talk with Lisa. She was the only one with enough authority and superior knowledge to whom I could talk. Maria I didn't trust; my other friends knew as little as I.

Lisa was lying on her bed in the upstairs bedroom she and Ellie shared. She was reading a magazine.

"Hi," I said in a manner to indicate that I wanted to talk to her.

"Mmmm," she said non-committally. I edged into her room. On the cover of the magazine she was reading I saw a picture of a couple embracing. The girl's eyes were closed, her cheek pressed against the man's face. Lisa saw me looking and snapped the magazine shut, the front cover face-down.

"What's that?" I asked with a face that reddened suddenly with the recall of Mr. Papetto's comic books.

"Nothing for you to see," she said. "What do you want?"

I shrugged. I didn't know exactly what I wanted to say, nor certainly how to say it.

"So get lost then." She placed her chin on her hands, gazing down on her rumpled pillow. Her light brown hair fell forward, hiding her face.

"You know that time that boy kissed you?"

Lisa rolled to her side and looked up at me. There was a distinct softening around her mouth, an indication she was willing to talk. I sat on the edge of her bed.

"Yeah?"

"What happens?" I seldom got my language to match the real images and questions inside my head.

"Happens?" She picked at her right eyebrow, a habit she had when thinking or upset. "I don't know. It's real nice."

"But I mean what happens? Does anything, you know, happen?"

"You mean something dirty?" Her eyes snapped indignation.

I was horrified. "No! God! What do you think?"

"Well, what do you mean, 'Does something happen?' and don't say, 'God!'" Her voice oozed with sarcasm. "You kiss, that's all. He puts his arms around you like this," she hugged herself in demonstration, "and you hug him back and then you put your lips together."

"Is it wet?"

"Oh, ick, wet!"

"Well, how should I know?" I wanted to tell her what I'd seen, but I felt ashamed now. The books were just dirty then; they had no connection to real people or events.

"Do you think people spit all over when they kiss?"

"No," I said, watching the tops of my tennis shoes as I rolled my toes up and down. "Maria Papetto showed me some books." I pointed to the magazine half-hidden beneath her. "Kind of like the one you have."

"You're too little to read them." She sat up. "And don't you tell anyone, or you'll get it."

"Then you're too little too!" I sing-songed. I was disappointed. If anyone could explain the nature of what I'd seen, Lisa could. But she was aloof now as she so often was, lording her superior knowledge and age over me. I left her room, ran down the stairs, and out the back door. I walked quickly, following the narrow dirt path that wound through the pines, through the woods, out into the tall sun-filled grass by the river. I sat on the large flat rocks that lined its banks and watched a water spider glide back and forth on its surface. This was something I was sure of, a world familiar and calm. A water spider revealed all of itself, its whole life and meaning perfectly evident. The world opened to me by Maria's father's tiny books was of a wholly different nature: it was secret and dark, connected to this blood that rushed to the surface whenever one of the images recalled itself. I wished I'd never seen them, and tried now to focus on the spider or the blue-winged dragonflies that darted nearby, but the images kept asserting themselves. I followed a bit of wood downcurrent under the bridge where the river turned noisy over the rocks there inside the echo created by the concrete walls. I'd been forbidden to ever go farther than this bridge beyond which the river curved out of sight. But I already had several times. And would again.

Two nights later Lisa and I got into an argument over the night-light in the hallway. I socked her hard without knowing why. The next morning she had a black eye. I wasn't sorry.

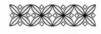

It is Saturday, May 14th, 1966, a magnificent day of blue sky and brisk air coming up the block and a half from the ocean to our small rented house. Ellie has come with her husband and young son to spend the day. They've driven down the California coast to this beach town where I live with my husband and three year old daughter. We've eaten the meal I prepared, a late afternoon affair, and settle now in the living room where we make conversation. Only three weeks have passed since Dad died and Ellie and I are both somewhat delicate with one another, less inclined toward pushing aside our sorrow with our family's brand of brazen humor.

We talk about Lisa. All of us, in varying degrees, are worried about her, and we discuss the possibility of her actually taking her life, a threat she has been making now for over a year. Until her recent move to Washington D.C., she has lived the last year or so with our parents. Dad, a pharmaceutical salesman, took her threats seriously enough to have gone over all his sample medicines and thrown out any that might serve her purpose. Mother helped him, so she too took Lisa's threats seriously.

But Lisa is often unhappy, Ellie and I explain to my husband who has not yet met her. We're used to that. From the time she was a child, she was given to pouts and tempers for reasons the rest of us could not discern. And she became very skilled at using her unhappiness to get us to do things for her or with her. I recall a specific moment in my late teens when Lisa asked me to go to a movie with her. Before I answered, I was perfectly aware that I did not want to go and that I was unable to say that to Lisa who sat curled in one corner of the sofa with her will directed at me. She was in no way pathetic; she didn't beg, but she created in me a sense of guilt as if I possessed something she never could, consequently owed her. And of course I did; I was essentially happy, basically pleased with myself. With Lisa, something was always wanting. So it worked: I said yes.

We, her sisters and our husbands, use all this to come to an uneasy conclusion that she will not do it. People who threaten suicide, we assure ourselves, never do it. It is with a sense of great relief when I return Ellie's beautiful smile as her husband pulls away from the curb, all of us waving, calling out, "Bye! Bye!"

I slipped out of bed and through the narrow space between my bed and Ellie's, careful not to bump hers. In the hallway I paused to listen for sounds of Tommy downstairs. There were only the refrigerator and the steady drip of the kitchen faucet.

With their creaks and groans, the stairs were impossible to sneak down until I discovered the sides were quietly solid. Then I moved quickly. I was suddenly afraid I'd overslept and my brother had left without me.

Tommy was waiting outside the bathroom door, one finger already to his lips to hush any reaction to the face he was making. I choked back a laugh. He made a worse face and rolled his eyes toward our parents' open door from which emerged Dad's loud snoring. We covered our mouths, but our laughter came out anyway, only distorted now into slightly obscene noises, making us laugh all the more. We rushed through the kitchen out the back door to gasp the cool air in relief. I signalled him to wait as I headed back inside.

"Hurry up," he whispered.

I found a sweater in the pile of clothes thrown on his dresser and hurried outside.

We ran down the slight slope of our yard into the long, wet grasses between the apple trees. Birds called and trilled. I was astonished at this dawn that emerged, wet and screaming, out of the night. Why had I never heard this racket before, why didn't the whole neighborhood wake up? Other than in the Hales' house, there were no lights on in any of the houses that lined the street.

When we reached the dirt driveway that encircled the Hales' farm we slowed to a walk.

The farm looked strange. The buildings had no real shadows yet, and everything was still in a way that felt like expectation. The familiarity made it all the stranger, as if I was moving in a dream. The chicken coops were empty as they had been all winter and the two large barns loomed uselessly, filled with abandoned tools and the fleeting odors of old gone things. An ancient tractor occupied the barn closest to our house. A relic. To Tommy and me, whose playground the Hales' farm had become, it was a dinosaur, far better than the bones downtown in the museum. We could climb this one, examine its every part.

My brother and I did not know that just ten years before all the coops had been filled, there had been several cows, and the empty fields at the far end of the farm had grown hay for the winter feed. The Hales were already old when we knew them. They had cut down on the work Mr. Hales could not do anymore even with Frank's help. Our own house and all the nearly identical houses lined up along the black tar road that was our neighborhood stood on land that had once grazed cows and grown corn and beans and tomatoes. (Just as I could not have seen that not far in the future, the Hales' house and those five or so acres of what was left of the original farm would be bought by the school board, all of this particular past swallowed up by a new junior high school with a six-foot chain link fence around the land's perimeters, one of whose edges was our property, by then of course in the hands of some other owner.) Selling one section of his farm to the contractor who had planned the monotonous row of small houses enabled Mr. Hales to let the cows go and most of the chickens. I knew none of this, that I was witness to the demise of one small Yankee farmer. I thought this was a farm, was how a farm should be, and delighted in the smells and feels of the various feeds, the soft mash and the cool, hard grains stored in wooden barrels in the feed shed where I spent after-noons talking with Frank.

"Oh. They're here." Tommy looked at me as if it were my fault. I ignored him.

"Look! They're white."

In the grey light, the flock of new chickens glowed, almost phosphorescent. They clustered nervously in the yard behind the two coops as Mr. Hales and the delivery man un-loaded the few chickens left on the truck. Tommy and I stood to one side, careful to keep out of the way. I was bursting to ask Mr. Hales if we could feed the birds this first morning. Mr. Hales never talked much, even when he was not busy, and I was afraid I'd spoil our chance if I spoke too soon. I imagined I had the discernment to know when the precisely right moment would arise.

Six hens were crammed inside one of the transport boxes, silent until Mr. Hales slid up the door and tilted the box to force them out. Then, wings flapping helplessly, feathers flying, they set up a hubbub of squawking. They scurried to the farthest corner of the yard, scattering the others as they broke paths for themselves, startling another roll of complaint among those both in the coop and in the yard.

There were two boxes left on the truck. One of these was filled with another six hens who were delivered with much the same results as before. The last box held only one bird, a large rooster. I had never seen such a creature. Alone, he almost filled the box. And though forced to squat back on his long yellow legs, so that his comb was crushed down at an absurd angle against the wooden slats, like a clown's hat, he asserted his dignity in the fierceness and disdain with which he glared at his human captors.

Even when the two men grabbed his box and the delivery man pushed him from behind, the rooster remained silent. He caught himself halfway down, his wings opened to break his fall. Instead of scattering nervously like the hens, he stood up tall, his neck outstretched as if to survey this new place and take in his present situation. He stood a moment like that, his head turning abruptly from one side to the other. Then he flapped his wings and stretched higher, shook himself and took one slow majestic step forward. The sun finally broke through the low clouds shooting warmth and light across the open fields. As though to apologize for his lateness, albeit due to circumstances beyond his control, the rooster cocked his head several times at the sun, then stretching up as high as he could, gave out a long, loud greeting to the sun.

"A king, just like a king," Tommy whispered.

I was still on the alert for the right time to ask about feeding the birds. Mr. Hales was talking in his quick, scratchy voice to the delivery man. To me, all adults were big, and their size relative to one another had no relevance normally, but Mr. Hales looked very small and thin this morning. Slightly stooped, his head inclined ahead of him as though he were moving forward even while standing still. He always wore a hat and I could never tell what color his hair was even though some of it showed from beneath the back rim of his hat. Frank's was white, as white as these chickens without the specks, but Mr. Hales' was somewhere between grey and brown. Like him. Somewhere between colors. Frank was knowable, like a tree. His eyes watered, but they looked straight at you out of their blue. Mr. Hales never looked at you. His eyes went to one side or the other as though your talking stopped him and he had to keep going so that his eyes kept on going for him. I was never comfortable with Mr. Hales. His laugh was the shadow of a laugh that had left. With such a laugh now, he put some money and papers on the seat of the truck. The big man picked them up and swung up onto the driver's seat. Tommy and I waited until the truck was making its turn into the driveway.

"Could we feed them, Mr. Hales?"

He bent toward me, his head to one side so his eyes could keep on moving. "Oh, not today. No, no. They're too nervous. Tomorrow maybe."

When disappointed, Tommy's eyes, deep brown like Mother's, always looked much sadder than my blue, or my Dad's hazel. I took a breath and insisted, "We'll be very careful and quiet."

"No, not today." He was already moving.

Mr. Hales disappeared into the coop, and Tommy and I settled in the grass to one side of the chicken yard. The hens, calmer now, nevertheless stayed far from where we sat. We couldn't get over their color. All the other chickens on the Hales' farm had been reddish-brown, and small in comparison. We decided these must be very special birds.

Mr. Hales appeared with a deep metal pail. He walked slowly through the yard, one hand dipping into the pail, rhythmically releasing a fistful of grain in a large half circle, the grain sparkling in the sunlight like water from a sprinkler. The chickens scattered away in a rush, then, as abruptly, rushed in to the area behind him that was now covered with grain. All the hens converged in a group together as though all of them wanted the exact same piece of corn. The larger hens always got their way, while the smaller ones ran frantically from one spot to the other taking quick pecks at what was left over. Feathers flying in the scramble for food, it was a wonder any of them had any feathers at all.

Mr. Hales left the yard through the outside door between the two long coops. We heard the pail clank as he dropped it, then saw him walk quickly down the driveway toward the house. He would eat breakfast now at the large dining room table covered with a lace tablecloth yellow with age. There would be that peculiar stale odor to the house which the Hales probably never noticed because they lived there.

There were five roosters in all. One looked old and scrawny, and two were young, still small. King was the largest, but there was one more almost as large, and certainly as beautiful and roosterly, as King.

"I bet he's a good fighter," Tommy remarked about King.

"I like that one over there better." I always went for the underdog. Tommy snickered.

"Look how he runs from King."

In their perusal of the yard, the two roosters had come within feet of one another. King rushed at the other bird who, while moving slowly to preserve a certain dignity, most definitely ran away.

"He's a chicken," Tommy sneered.

"He is not," I protested and we both laughed. "I mean he *is* a chicken, but not a *chicken*," I insisted.

"Let's call him Mortimer," my brother suggested.

In the days that followed, the chickens grew used to our presence by the fence. They even gathered near us to take the succulent grass we extended through the wire. I loved the long, low sounds the hens made when they were content, or their loud indignant scolding when angry or disturbed. There was no sound more indignant than a hen's. They even looked indignant the way they held their heads and peered down their beaks with their fierce eyes. On hot afternoons, they scratched out shallow holes in the dry earth, and lowered themselves into these as if into a tub, kicking up the loose surface dirt into their feathers, shaking their wings and tail feathers to distribute the dust through what looked like layers of ruffled white petticoats.

But the fierce-looking King and Mortimer provided the drama. King sometimes herded a few hens into a group and then, as if he had done it simply to show he was boss, would stretch up, neck extended, and crow loudly three or four times. Satisfied with his display of power, he would strut around the yard.

When Mortimer tried to do the same, King would hurry to the gathering hens and scatter them, then give chase to Mortimer. Mortimer kept his distance from King, but continued in this way to challenge his dominance. Clearly, the chicken yard could have only one boss. And clearly that boss was King. The three other roosters kept close to the edges of the yard and crowed only occasionally.

Gradually Tommy lost interest and stopped going to watch the chickens with me. So I was alone this day, on my way toward the chicken yard, when I heard the single, sharp sound of an angry bird. I ran. In front of the yard door between the two coops, the hens were gathered in a semi-circle, all facing the same way, watching something, completely silent. Suddenly, from behind their white mass, King rose up, his neck curved gracefully like a scimitar. He too was silent except for the sound his beak made when it struck.

I rushed around the one long coop and into the shadowed space between the two. Through the slatted door, I could just see Mortimer. He lay on his belly, his head tucked down into his shoulders, his white neck and breast splashed red with the blood from his comb. I thought he was dead, but he flinched when King's deadly beak struck him again. I could not understand why he lay there like that, nor why King continued to attack when Mortimer's defeat was obvious. But I did understand the hens' silent intensity. They were waiting for King to kill Mortimer. Mortimer was waiting too. He made no sound even when fresh blood was drawn.

The roosters were a few feet from the door. Improvising, I lifted the latch and threw it open. King looked at me. An alarm rose up among the hens, but none moved. Instead they also fastened their attention on me. I grabbed the rake just inside the door and shook it at King. He backed off. The hens in front startled and turned, pushing against the others behind them. But their line held and, as though assessing my capacity, King started toward me. Again I threatened him with the rake; this time he retreated further. As a last resort, I threw the rake at King, took the few steps to Mortimer and scooped him up in my arms. He had not moved.

As one, the flock began to move toward me, their protests growing. I fled the yard, just managing to pull the door closed. The chickens were milling around behind me; King actually hurled himself up against the flimsy door once or twice. By now, I was trembling, but I was also filled with amazement—at my feat, my success, at this bird in my arms, how light he was, his body all feathers, nothing much but bones underneath—when I remembered Dad's and Mr. Hales' warnings about roosters, and my amazement dissolved. Mortimer could turn on me. He was a rooster after all. Ready to drop him at the first sign of struggle, I walked as quickly as my now-jellied legs could take me to one of the small coops. There I gently placed him on the floor.

I settled outside at the wide wire window. Mortimer remained on his breast, his eyes half-closed, as though still await-ing the final blow. When it didn't come, his eyes opened wider, then wide, first to take in me for several long moments, then his new surroundings. Slowly he stood up, looked around and shook himself. Blood from his comb splattered all around, some of it on my t-shirt.

"You're going to be all right now, Mortimer." He watched me with one cold eye. I spoke softly to soothe him.

As I returned from the feed shed, I saw him pacing the tiny coop, a dethroned prince lonely for his kingdom. But he also looked somewhat recovered. He held his head high again, not ducked down into his shoulders. I went cautiously into the coop and placed the food in an old tin bowl in one dusty corner. Since he neither ran from me nor at me, I risked sitting on the roosting bar inside the coop. When, at last, he began to eat, I felt the way I knew Mother felt on those occasions one of us was sick and the fever finally broke. Once we heard King crow in the distant yard. Mortimer's head shot up from the bowl. He peered out the wire window for a long time.

I stayed with Mortimer the rest of the afternoon. Gradually, he got used to my closeness and, after a few jabs at me, allowed me to pet his soft neck feathers and feed him grain out of my hand. The whole time I was trying to figure out the right approach to get Mr. Hales to agree to let him stay where he was, and mainly, to let Mortimer be mine. Toward dinnertime, I ran up to their house. I explained what had happened, exaggerating to get Mr. Hales' sympathy. He chuckled at the story, and looked off into the distance.

"I guess he can stay there. He's no good in the yard."

"I'll take care of him, Mr. Hales. You won't have to bother about him. Would that be okay?" I was sure he understood that I was asking him to give me Mortimer as my own. Mr. Hales just nodded, still far away, wherever he went with those eyes of his.

"Do you suppose he could have a few hens to keep him company?"

This time he really looked at me, straight on, and gave a real laugh. But he did not answer.

I walked Mortimer in the open area surrounded by the driveway, a string looped around one leg like a leash, but soon I just let him go where he wanted. If he went too far, I would stand in front of him, forcing him to turn back. I liked to think he was walking with me.

Within a short time, his comb healed and he looked as big and healthy as King. I was very proud of him and of my association with him. We understood one another. Not through my words which I knew were nonsense to him. Not even through my act that had saved him. I could not have explained why I believed this understanding was real, I simply knew it existed, and not only in me as a supposedly superior creature but in Mortimer as well. Even then I suspected the human view of humanity as superior to all others to be not only self-serving and arrogant, but also as opinion posing as fact. Mortimer trusted me. He may indeed even have loved me in whatever way a chicken might love. In any case, he was as wonderful a pet as any dog might be. Excited to see me each day when I arrived, he turned quiet when I got ready to leave, and watched me go for as long as he could see me with one large questioning eye. He listened carefully to everything I said, turning his head to examine me first with one eye, then the other.

One hot Saturday, my parents announced we would all go to the beach the next day; early, since it was over an hour's drive on the hot, tarry roads. I managed to get up early enough to go feed Mortimer. The heat of the day was already intense and I looked forward to the cool, ocean air, the only cloud in my particular sky the fact that Mortimer would be left alone so long.

I splashed and played in the salty water all day. Only once did I sit on the sand and that was when my parents insisted that I rest for a while after eating the sun-warmed tuna sandwich Mother had brought. When we got back that night, I was too tired to go over to the Hales'. The salt of the water left its trails on my skin, I could still hear the ocean waves and air like a lullaby that made me heavy with sleep. I went to bed right after the light supper Mother prepared.

The next morning the coop was empty. Small white feathers lay unmoving on the floor as though they had been there for years. A few clung to the wire window and trembled in the air. I ran to the big yard, then from coop to coop to see if Mr. Hales had moved Mortimer. He was nowhere to be found.

Monday was shopping day for the Hales, the one day of the week they backed the shiny old black car out of the garage, whose doors stood wide open now onto the emptiness within. I banged on their door anyway. No one answered. I was hot, the heat in my face which I knew would be red. I walked slowly home kicking up dust with the toes of my shoes.

Dad had not yet left for work. Though he was surprised at Mortimer's disappearance, his eyes revealed that he somehow knew where he had gone. There was that peculiar gentleness in them that I recognized from the time our puppy had died.

"Mr. Hales is a farmer," was all he said.

Lisa was in the room.

"Sunday chicken," she said, and blushed when my father shot her a sharp look.

I went into the back bedroom and lay on the sofa bed. After a while Lisa came in and sat on the edge.

"You know those new paper dolls I got?"

I just looked at her.

"Want to help me cut them out?"

They were the kind of dolls that came with cardboard stands so you didn't have to lay them down. I hesitated. Though I had my own book of uncut dolls, Lisa's was prettier, and she and Ellie never asked me to cut out dolls with them. My feelings of grief became confused with a certain amazement at this new status that Mortimer's disappearance had given me. I nodded. She didn't even criticize me when I cut off the corners of the flaps or high heels. The next day when I confidently joined her to continue the game, she glared at me.

"Look at these." She held up the dresses I had cut out. White lines edged parts of the tops, the flaps were rounded, other details cut off entirely. "Go play with your own." Her disgust was obvious.

That weekend my father brought home a pair of pigeons. I named them Pete and Maggie and spent hours sitting in the coop Dad spent all of Saturday building for them in the corner of the garage. Ellie and Lisa called me Pigeon Girl. I didn't care. I preferred real birds to paper dolls anyway. In a few weeks there were a couple of smooth eggs in the nest. It turned out that Pete was the mother, Maggie the father.

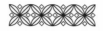

It was the middle of the night. We were sleeping. But the thumping woke us and my husband went to the door. All the bad news I'd been getting during my father's illness had come by telegram—we had no phone—so knocking at the door brought me tensely awake. My husband came back to bed complaining about some fool who had the wrong address. I relaxed and sank back into sleep.

Who knows how much later it was; fifteen, twenty minutes, and then the pounding at the door again. It was like a nightmare, the man who pursues, will not let you go, he's there again, after you thought you'd escaped, pounding down the door. You know he'll get you sooner or later. This time I went. A short, warmly-jacketed man held out the familiar yellow envelope. He made the mistake again, it was the name, the way he was pronouncing our last name, maybe he couldn't see it in the dark, but I figured out that it was the right address and, looking at the spelling, I saw how, yes, it was intended for me.

What now? I don't know that I even thought that. I remember that the man looked relieved, he'd been right all along, this was the house. I opened the envelope, then the folded telegram inside. Perhaps I expected something about my mother, more likely I just held my breath, but what I saw there, the words that laid themselves out, knocked all breath out of me.

Lisa is dead. Stop. Call or come tomorrow.

Lisa is dead. How else to say it? The telegram was from Ellie who had left our home hours before. My brother had been trying to reach her half the day. For her the words had to be that accurate, *Lisa is dead.* There was no way to dress it up. It was precisely what she had to say.

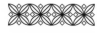

My sisters rarely gave my parents any trouble. Singly, neither did my brother nor I. Together, however, was a different story.

We let the neighbors' chickens and rabbits out of their pens; we threw mud balls on Mother's sheets hung out to dry, brought home stray or wounded animals which we then hid so we'd be able to keep them. One was a descented skunk which poor Mother discovered in the cold room down in the basement. She did not know, of course, that it was either descented or tame.

Twice, we set fire to a house. The first was our own, which could have burned down had my father not figured out that we'd done something by the way we joined him and Mother to sit quietly in the summer cool of the apple tree, then seen the smoke. In the few minutes since I'd dropped the match and run, the fire had spread quickly, fed by the fuel of the Sunday newspaper. He grabbed my doll's blanket, the nearest thing at hand, and beat at the flames licking up the curtains on the living room window. For years, the yellowed and blistered paint remained to remind me of my first attempts, at Tommy's urging, to light a match. The second time was our next door neighbor's house where, in an experiment gone awry, the basement stairs exploded into flames with us and two other kids trapped in the basement. That time, we managed to beat the fire out ourselves.

Something between us triggered not only our imaginations, but our daring and willingness to do things that, alone, neither would even consider. Parental borders evaporated in the fever of our combined appetites to try out the world. Mother was patient, even surreptitiously encouraging in the way she shook her head at our latest mischief with a barely suppressed smile or look of appreciative pride in her eyes. The weekdays alone with us she usually just let us go, hoping we'd survive, along with the neighborhood.

Dad, however, did not consider our antics amusing. His eyes revealed, not humor, but a concentrated determination to scare the bejeezus out of us, probably so he could have the peaceful evenings and weekends he so longed for, and rarely got. So when Great Aunt Sue died, and Mother had to attend the funeral, it was decided that one of us had to go. My father could not be left in charge of my brother and me together. And I was easier for Mother than Tommy whose dancing, deep brown eyes were so much like her own. So I was chosen.

I hardly knew my Aunt Sue. We had visited her home on Long Island perhaps two times. She was crippled by something that kept her in a wheelchair, so our Great Uncle Dick did the running around. They had a Boston bull terrier which they adored and, because Tommy and I also adored him, we found a place in Uncle Dick's and Aunt Susie's hearts that we might not otherwise have occupied. As we sat on the floor between Uncle Dick and his dog, full of questions about the little dog, it was clear that he had to tear himself away from us in order to serve the others. Our admiration of the dog made him laugh and turn pink with pleasure. Besides the dog, he had a world globe in his study upstairs. Something of a geography buff, he also delighted in sharing it with us. Between the dog and the globe, my brother and I were kept busy and happy.

But for everyone else, the visits seemed difficult, uncomfortable. We all had to dress up, as though for church, and Lisa and Ellie were captives in their navy outfits, bows in their hair, trying not to scuff their patent leather shoes, politely responsive to Aunt Sue's well-mannered questions and comments. With a cloud of bluish-white hair above her dazzling smile and serious brown eyes, Aunt Sue seemed like a fairy godmother, or princess, in whose presence one dare not quite relax.

Now, on the train down to New York, as we headed for the funeral, Mother kept reminding me how I'd better behave myself. Her admonishments were unnecessary. Both the hush of her voice when she referred to Aunt Sue's death, along with my brother's absence, assured my good behavior.

At the funeral parlor, an overpowering odor, sweet and sticky, met us at the door, together with a stranger in black who held Mother's hand too long, and took the liberty of pulling me toward him in a tender hug. Ours was not a family for touching. Embraces and kisses occurred only at arrivals or departures after or preceding long absences, and were always awkward, dreaded in advance, discharged quickly and with as little contact as possible. So for a stranger to touch me and look directly, with sympathy-ladened eyes, into mine aroused real alarm.

Mother guided me into the room where Aunt Sue was laid out. I'd never seen a dead person, but Mother had made it clear that mere curiosity would appear crass. So I sank to my knees beside her in one of the pews, bowed my head, as she did, and moved my lips in prayer as I stole glimpses of the casket and my surroundings.

All around were my aunts and uncles, a few cousins, and my grandmother, people I knew well but scarcely recognized with these newly-hushed voices and reddened eyes. Uncle Dick and my grandmother, along with other relatives I did not know on Aunt Sue's side, sat in a row up front. Strangers and relatives kept going up to one or another of them, leaning toward them to say something in whispers. I wanted Mother to tell me what I was supposed to say, but she had her head bowed into her hands.

"Come on," she whispered suddenly, taking my elbow. She guided me out the pew and toward the front row where the ordeal of greeting was modulated by the palpable sorrow of the mourners. Grandma, always lively with interest or amusement at what was happening around her, focussed briefly on me when she hugged me, then went vague as she returned to some inner territory that clearly had her attention. Only when she recognized my mother did her face light up with its typical attentiveness.

"Betty! Oh, my dear." Her teeth clicked delicately with each syllable, the loose upper plate slipping, as it always did. Odd that none of us children ever laughed about this, even behind Grandma's back. Here she was, her teeth rattling around in her mouth like a joke skeleton's; yet her dignity remained as absolute as the white of her hair.

"Mom." My mother's voice broke as she and Grandma embraced with real feeling. Aunt Susie was Grandma's sister.

"Kneel up there and say a prayer for Aunt Susie," Mother said in my ear, giving me a delicate shove towards the casket. I balked; she pushed me harder.

"Aren't you coming too?"

She heard the pleading and took my hand. Together we knelt on the padded kneelers. I could hardly breathe with the heady perfume of the flowers. And when I'd just gotten up enough courage to look at Aunt Sue, I felt the wake of Mother's body as she got up and moved away. Her place was filled by Uncle Dick. I watched him press Susie's hand, saw how her flesh indented slightly from the pressure of his fingers, and did not spring back. I heard him murmur, "Oh she's cold. My God, she's cold," and felt a chill on my own arms in my short-sleeved dress, noticed now something different about Aunt Sue, how she seemed to have more in common with the fabric of her dress than with the person she still resembled. She wasn't Aunt Sue anymore, but here was Uncle Dick whispering to her, touching her, as though any moment he could awaken her. And, in fact, the benign and gentle look of her face encouraged such a notion. I had just dared to look at her face when I felt myself being led away.

Mother made eye contact with me. "You stay here now and be good."

"But where are you going?" The room she was leading me into was dimly lit and furnished exactly like the one across the hall, except the space between the two pillars occupied by Aunt Sue in the other room was empty here. I was not brave when it came to things like this. I was afraid of the dark, vulnerable to a vivid imagination that saw shadowy creatures in every corner. Having seen the film *Frankenstein* six months before, I was still having terrible nightmares and would continue to have them for two more years. This was not a room I wanted to be in, even when I made out that two of my cousins were already there.

"Now, now," Mother said. "I'm just going downstairs. I won't be long."

"Let me come," I clung to her hand.

"No, you can't. Downstairs is only for adults. Children aren't allowed."

I wondered what could be worse downstairs than where I was now. From what followed I later realised there was either a bar where mourners could dispel their sorrow, or a lounge where they could bring their own spirits for the same purpose. But I assumed, and by her tone and behavior Mother encouraged my thinking in this direction, that there was something terrible down there.

Mother greeted my cousins Trudy and Anne as she led me to a chair next to Trudy. Trudy was my favorite cousin, yet neither of us dared even to say hello once Mother left; the three of us sat rigidly upright, intent upon every shadow.

We sat like that for a long time, staring hard at the velvet draperies behind the pillars, our ears atuned to any possible sound within the room. For me, this was worse than any ghost story I'd ever heard. I was in this one.

Anne started to say something.

"Shhh!" Trudy commanded.

I looked at the curtains again. Surely, anything that might show up would come from there.

Trudy turned her head tensely from one side to the other, her eyes big.

"What?" I finally dared to whisper.

"What's that?" she asked urgently.

We listened. While voices, gayer and louder than before, reached us from below, our room was silent.

"It's nothing," Anne said with a sneer.

"Shhh!" Trudy insisted. The youngest of us three, she had an air of authority about her. She was the oldest of five in her mother's growing brood of children. Anne was an only child. I was the youngest of four.

"I'm going downstairs." I slipped off my chair.

"Sit down," she ordered. I sat. "It's gone now." This was said matter-of-factly.

"What was it?"

Anne gave me a look that told me just how stupid she thought I was. "Nothing," she sneered. "She's always doing stuff like that. Big faker."

Trudy was not easily baited. "Probably it was nothing," she said calmly.

The sound of singing, first soft, then louder with the voices off-key and out-of-sync, began to rise into the upstairs hall.

"Here they go." Trudy rolled her eyes in mock disapproval.

What I most admired about Trudy was her big-city cynicism, her knowing airs. Even with adults, she could hold her own without getting smart-alecky or silly. Adults listened to her, actually took her seriously. In my experience, that was unheard-of, in my own family and in my friends'. Uncle Brian and Aunt Sal treated Trudy as an equal, with respect. Perhaps because, other than Grandma who lived with them and took care of the housework and cooking while my aunt and uncle worked, Trudy, at eight years of age, was mother to her younger sisters and brothers. She was boss. What she said was law. She apparently never abused that and took good care of the little ones, as the other children were collectively called. And apparently had her fill of it, for, when she grew up and married, she chose to have no children of her own.

We inched our chairs back to peer across the hall. In the other room, Uncle Dick was bent forward, his elbows on his knees, his hands over his face. Grandma sat very still beside him, hands cupped softly in her lap, her large brown eyes softened by sorrow, and appearing larger, darker, due to the halo of pure white hair that set them off.

As the singing below grew louder, however, Grandma sat straighter, her head tilted toward the hall with a frown of puzzlement. Though she could not yet hear the words, familiar Irish tunes lilted upward, wisps of joviality rising against the overwhelming presence of death, as if life were the ghost here, oddly out of place. Accompanying the songs was the drone of a single voice whose message could not be deciphered but which concluded in a peal of laughter.

"They're telling jokes now," Trudy announced. "Let's see if we can hear."

Slipping off our chairs, we went to the door and stationed ourselves on either side. The head, then trunk, of Uncle Brian, rose out of the stairwell. His face was the reddest in a family whose men tended toward red faces, and his blue eyes shone brilliantly in contrast. The smile that suffused his face when he first emerged had, by the top of the stairwell, evaporated. The jauntiness of his step, the lightness that had carried him upward, slowed and became visibly weighted. He took a few moments to pull at his jacket and tie, run his hands through his hair, and adjust his posture so that he stood erect and dignified. He then entered the room that held Aunt Sue. Leaning solicitously over Grandma, he whispered something. Her face became alert, she shook her head and indicated her brother-in-law quietly moaning and rocking back and forth in his chair. Uncle Brian placed an arm around Dick's shoulder and spoke quietly to him. Lowering his hands to listen, Dick nodded a few times, then stared at the floor in front of him. Uncle Brian crossed the hall and entered our room.

"You girls okay?" His voice conveyed infinite gentleness, every word softened as though rounded in upon itself. Not like any man's voice I'd ever heard.

"Can we come downstairs, Daddy?" Trudy asked.

"That's for the adults, honey." Uncle Brian held down two jobs. Days he was a cop, nights a security guard. But there was never menace in his voice, never the sharpness I heard in my own father's, filled with an angry impatience that was so often directed at my brother and me.

A pair of high heels thumped heavily up the stairs.

"Hey, Brian, come on," Aunt Kate called out when she saw him, "we need you down here."

Grandma's head shot up, she darted a look of anger at her oldest daughter who grimaced toward the other room after Uncle Brian put a finger to his lips.

Kate stifled her laugh and whispered loudly. "Hi girls. You all okay up here?" Trudy and I giggled at the way her words seemed to gyrate as if her tongue were twisted into the shape of a corkscrew.

"Come on there, fella," Kate continued in her loud whisper, "we need you. No one knows the words." She pulled herself up the last few stairs and stood a moment to catch her breath. "Oh my," she huffed, "that's quite a haul."

Trudy and I doubled over and Kate joined us with a laughter she attempted to smother, making us laugh all the harder.

Brian sensed the situation was getting out of control. Glances of outrage were shot toward the hallway from the handful of elderly mourners.

"Gotta go, girls. You be good now."

He took Aunt Kate's arm at the top of the stairs. "Easy now," he said, "we don't want you to break a leg."

Kate exploded with a breathless laughter.

"What is it?" someone called from downstairs.

"Oh!" Kate burst out over and over in a rich soprano as she attempted to catch her breath. "He doesn't want me to fall," she finally managed to say.

Brian was trying to hush her, but she had the kind of voice that, even when lowered, carried into every corner. "Well, we're certainly in the right place, I'll say," she stage-whispered. "They can just lay me out next to Susie."

Ohs! of shock, Kates! of horror, My goodnesses! of embarrassment were quickly swallowed by a hearty irreverant laughter from those below.

Uncle Dick suddenly appeared in the hallway. He was pale. "Have you no respect?"

Brian shrugged helplessly as he attempted to wrestle Aunt Kate down the stairs.

Uncle Dick faced back into the room where his wife lay. He shouted, "You see? That's what you get marrying common Irish!" He directed this at my grandmother.

"Common Irish?" Kate's voice rose an octave and sharpened. "Did that old goat say common Irish?" Her face poked up where we could see her again. Her eyes flashed, and from the way her head bobbed up and down, it was clear those below were trying to get her back downstairs.

"I don't give a damn," we heard now from below as she disappeared. Uncle Dick closed the curtained French doors that led into the room where Aunt Susie lay. His shadow slid down the curtain and moved away.

Aunt Kate's voice reverberated in the upstairs hall. "A lucky man he is Pop isn't alive to hear that, God rest his soul. I'll say."

"Lace curtain Irish," a female voice intoned with feeling, voicing a class defense for the slur of being called 'common Irish,' the distinction, important only to the Irish themselves, that of the upper class 'lace curtain' and lower-born 'shanty' Irish.

"The old Kraut!" Kate's voice called out, followed by hushes all around. Uncle Dick was German; his family had immigrated from Germany, as had my grandmother's own family albeit with a suspiciously Italian-sounding last name. The word 'kraut' landed in the upstairs hall.

We watched the curtained doors. Dick did not appear.

Things quieted a bit, then a raucous laughter burst out, accompanied by the stomping of feet. Someone began to sing, "If you knew Susie, like I knew Susie."

All three of us huddled by the door trying to catch every word, enjoying the scandal, unaware this was a scandal, when the door across the hall opened. Grandma was a tiny woman, less than five feet tall, and bent over even smaller by her widow's hump. She had never weighed more than ninety-five pounds in her life. For all that, her appearance at this moment loomed large as she walked quickly to the bannister.

"Katherine," she called down. "Katherine McGee, you get up here this instant."

We heard another stifled burst of laughter.

"Mom? Is that you, Mom?" Aunt Kate called out.

"You get Joe to call me a taxi right now. I have never been so ashamed in my life. For God's sake, my own sister."

The merriment audibly fizzled. The voices turned quiet and serious, and one by one my aunts and uncles and mother emerged up the stairway, their faces flushed with the previous gaity, their eyes averted like chastened children. Mother wouldn't look at me though I tried to catch her eye. I wanted her to acknowledge I wasn't the only one who got into trouble. Mother did not awaken me the next morning to attend the ceremony in the church and cemetery. I was not sorry to miss it, especially when I heard that just as they were going to lower Aunt Sue into the ground, a strong wind came up, bringing rain, thunder and bolts of lightning that sent the mourners scurrying for shelter. It was just what I had expected the night before, what I was afraid I'd have to witness there in that dim room alone with my cousins, what I assumed any good Catholic got when she died. Signs. God Himself. A real send-off.

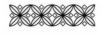

I would find this out later:

On Friday, May 13th, at around dinnertime, Ellie's phone rang. Picking it up, she heard only the sound of breathing. Not the mash call sort, just slow breathing, and Ellie felt the impulse to say, "Lisa?" Reason intervened. "Hello? Hello?" she said instead. When no one responded she hung up.

None of us can be sure, but the time was about right. And Ellie was Lisa's closest friend. Did Lisa call to hear her sister's voice for the last time? To try to get a message through in order to be saved but was already too far gone? This was one of the questions I wanted an answer to, one of the things I held Lisa responsible for. If she called just to hear Ellie's voice, she had no right, I thought. No right to do that. But if she called for help, that was terrifying. I kept choosing the first. It fed my anger, kept at least that one door closed.

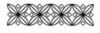

Being a girl was the last thing I wanted to be. But girl I was. So one steamy September afternoon when everyone was away, I dragged my bed, piece by piece, upstairs to my sisters' room where I reassembled it smack in the middle, between theirs. Until then, I'd slept in my brother's room.

I was still wrestling the awkward mattress up the stairs when Mother and my sisters returned from downtown, hot but happy, with several bags filled with new school clothes. When they saw what I was doing, they all got quiet. Mother laughed nervously, my sisters said nothing. No one offered to help. They took the bags into the kitchen instead of opening them there in the living room as they would have normally. Even then, I didn't hear the usual rattling of paper and happy cries of "Look at this!"

I was eleven years old. The whole family knew the time was overdue for me to move upstairs, but our house was small, the rooms barely able to contain us all, so no doubt the hope had been that I would remain the carefree tomboy, unfazed by my sexually neuter role. If I could have obliged them, I would have.

To enter the female world was, to me, the equivalent of entering jail. I wasn't stupid. I'd observed the lives of girls and women. Girls played games that kept them close to home: variations on ball games, jump rope, hopscotch; girls got teased with insects, snakes, having their skirts pulled up; they sat around the house, or under trees engrossed by their dolls or tiny tea sets; they helped wash dishes and iron, made beds and cookies. There was nothing wrong with any of this: I did all of it. But I also ran in the woods, swam in the river, caught frogs and bugs, climbed trees, made base hits, came home on a regular basis wet, torn up, or bruised.

I had no desire to be a boy; I loved being a girl—at least the girl I was. But I wanted none of the generic girl world. That I despised. I even had a secret game I played to torture myself about being a conventional girl. No one knew about this game, not even Tommy: I was a girl whose father would not allow her to leave the yard, who had to dress up nicely, and stay clean. No friends were good enough for her, she was lonely and sad. To play the game, I'd get a bright pink rubber ball—the kind all the neighbor girls played with—and pace up and down our sidewalk, bouncing the ball in ways that displayed frustration, anger, or resignation, as I told an imaginary visiting cousin of all the restrictions my father put on me. My cousin would shake her head, awed at my heroic compliance in the face of such limitations. To her, I was a kind of saint. The game was a personal variation on the fairy tales of imprisoned princesses. It expressed both my horror and fascination with the role of the female.

But, by eleven, the jig was up. Various pressures were on me to change. The word 'tomboy' was no longer said, as it always had been, with amused admiration or, at the worst, a tolerant disdain. Now it took on a mysterious menace. And though the menace itself was never made clear, the consequences were: I was no longer acceptable the way I was; I had to become a girl in every sense of the word.

So moving my bed was no victory. Everyone in the family was aware of its meaning to me, its signalling of submission, particularly Mother who was the one, I believe, who most enjoyed watching my childhood freedom, who egged both me and my brother on in our pursuits of mischief and adventure. Something in her nature yearned for what she made sure I got. Outwardly she was the most passive of women, tending her home and her family's every need. But beneath that conventional facade, squashed down to fit, was a woman puzzled and angered by the drudgery of her daily life.

My sisters' beds were matching twins, maroon-painted wood with four low posters, tucked under the sloped ceiling. I had to first move their beds to the longer window wall in order to make room for mine. Mine was higher, and metal, with a tall headrest that had always made a perfect steed on which I rode my pillow saddle, a rope around the short post, a steed I no longer rode once I moved upstairs. The only place my bed looked good was exactly where I'd put it—between theirs. The room was balanced then, if wall-to-wall beds can be considered in the light of balance or aesthetics.

Moving upstairs was not only a surrender, however, it was also a declaration. Two months before, the family had taken a trip to visit a great aunt in her summer home on Chesapeake Bay. On the way, we stopped for one night to stay with another great aunt whose home was not much larger than our own. My mother and two sisters were to sleep together in one room; my father, brother, and me in another. I remember protesting, probably because it was the first time I was so clearly separated out from the women in the family, and then in front of a virtual stranger.

At home, it seemed perfectly natural to share my brother's room. We would whisper to each other from our separate beds, giggling about the day's exploits, or planning the next day's, until Dad stormed down the hall to threaten us with outrageous punishments—"You won't eat in this house for a week!" "I'll never take you skating again!"—unless we settled down and went to sleep.

But, at Great Aunt Gert's, it suddenly felt peculiar. It was as if I was not acknowledged as a girl, or that it did not matter that I was in the way it mattered with Ellie and Lisa. Certainly they were older—fourteen and sixteen—but I was eleven, I had reached a border.

Mother saw my distress and actually showed me the tiny room she, Ellie and Lisa would share so I would understand why

I was being shoved in with the boys. But she also let me know I ought not to make a fuss, this being in her Aunt Gert's house, and how we were imposing.

I was furious. Dad gave me the choice of the floor or the bed, he didn't care, but he was getting the bed with either my brother or me since he had the long drive tomorrow and needed his sleep. I chose the bed.

My brother settled down on the pile of blankets in the narrow space between the wall and the bed. I stretched out luxuriously on the double bed. Dad was with Mother and Aunt Gert in the living room. I stretched out further, forming myself into a V shape, my feet pushed up against the wall so that I took up at least three quarters of the bed space.

My anger had not dissipated. Why should I be treated as if I were not like Ellie and Lisa? What was wrong with me?

I heard the grown-ups saying their good-nights. Without thought, a plan formed.

Dad came into the room. I remained in my V-position, my eyes closed, breathing as though I were in a deep sleep. I heard him undressing in the dark, then felt the gentle nudge against my back as he tried to push me to my side of the bed. I breathed naturally, deeply.

"Barbara," he whispered. He tried again to nudge me over. I resisted, but kept my breathing normal.

He said something quietly, under his breath, and I heard him then as he took his pillow from the bed, and settled down on the floor at its foot.

I was amazed. I couldn't believe I'd pulled it off. The next morning, the event simply became one of our family stories. Dad, red-eyed and sleepy from a bad night's rest, laughed ruefully about how I was sound asleep and just wouldn't move.

It was after this trip that I began agitating to move upstairs. My demand was not rejected, though Lisa's scowls let me know how she felt about it; it was just constantly put off by vagueness about when this would happen, or how. I saw that the only way I was going to get there was with a *fait accompli*. I had been waiting two full months for the day when I would have the house to myself.

Beneath my bravado, that apparently brazen act of asserting myself between my sisters, I was afraid of how they would receive me, particularly Ellie. She was so different from me: first, those insurmountable five years that put her at such a distance, then her quiet centeredness. Where Tommy and I spent most of our days outdoors, Ellie seemed to spend hers indoors, legs tucked elegantly beneath her on the sofa or a chair, reading. Or she'd disappear with her friends. Oh, she did things outdoors too, like swim, sunbathe, or skate, but with that same ladylike demureness, a reserve I had assumed indicated mere tolerance of Tommy and me.

Lisa was also different, but in a less intimidating way. She seemed to vascillate between actual enjoyment of my brother's and my company—as when she told us stories or came to pick violets or dogwood down in the woods with us—and irritation at our being so young and foolish enough to be almost constantly in trouble with Dad. Every evening, Ellie and Lisa sat across the dinner table from us, Mother at one end, Dad at the other. Their side emanated quiet, a dignified obedience. Tommy's and my side seemed jittery in contrast: we were rebels, disliking our food, always on the verge of disruption, even when we tried to behave or manage to swallow the dreaded liver or codfish cakes.

So moving upstairs was like moving in to a new neighborhood. Though we shared parents, home and history, I didn't really know my sisters. Tommy I knew. He was like another self. We were nearly inseparable. My parents I knew the way children know parents, not as people so much as functions: disciplinarian, protector, storyteller, driver, listener, dinner's ready caller, ice skating pond maker, orange juice squeezer. My sisters I knew scarcely at all.

Once there, between them, I felt defensive. I had the right to be there, I knew that, and knew they knew, but I was also keenly aware of my intrusion. Physically, we were jammed together, the spaces between our beds scarcely wide enough to move through sideways, the space at the foot, big enough for only two of us at a time, what with the chests of drawers. All three of us were immoderately modest and took turns dressing or undressing behind the hall closet door just outside the room. The bathroom was downstairs. Mornings could be treacherous if one of us got up late and the hall was occupied.

"I won't look, I promise. Please let me by."

Even in our slips we all felt naked. And of course this modesty became no small weapon that we used one against the other during those crucial morning hours.

To my surprise, Ellie accepted my arrival without complaint. She even made me feel comfortable by acting and talking in ways I assumed to be normal. I'd expected sly remarks, coded exchanges, private laughter, name-calling even. Nothing like that occurred. Lisa, however, was sullen for weeks, complaining loudly about my invasion, and why didn't I just stay downstairs where I belonged. At fourteen, she was constantly unhappy about clothes—nothing fit, nothing looked good, her older sister always got the best. She couldn't complain about me; I wore the hand-me-downs. She would plead for a certain dress or outfit and if she finally got it, complained then about its color or fabric or style. What she could not face was that the problem was her: she was overweight. No one was allowed to point that out.

Moving upstairs marked the end of my childhood. It was not a bad ending, just, as endings go, a time of confusion and change as ending spirals into beginning. My sisters were already girls in every way, but also in ways I hadn't seen or expected. They were funny and witty, daring in ways different from Tommy and me, but daring nevertheless. Ellie stayed pretty much undercover, keeping herself to herself, but, through her love of study, graduated with honors, thereby paving the way to college for the rest of us. And Lisa began to do amazing things as soon as she entered high school. She ran for student council, class secretary, hall monitor, making her own election signs at home, writing her own speeches, and was elected to all of them. I stopped judging the feminine in such negative ways and if I did not embrace the limitations put upon girls and young women back in the Fifties, I stopped torturing myself with them. A girl was what I had to shape myself into and my sisters became important models. I wasn't like them, but they weren't like each other either. It was a great relief to discover that being female was not so generic as I'd thought. I crossed the border, made it to the other side.

I no longer recall why my husband and I decided not to have a phone. It was not the money I don't think, but I cannot remember what idealized reasons we invented for ourselves. It was a terrible disability, however. When my father first became ill, I was sent telegrams to call home. This meant going down a half a block to a phone booth next to a liquor store. Then, with a dread that grew over the months, I would make my call and get the ever-worsening news.

Two and a half weeks after my father's death, I called Ellie to confirm that she and her family were coming to lunch that Saturday. During the conversation, she told me distressing news: Lisa was pregnant. Thirty, unmarried, in love with the man whose child she was carrying, but who, apparently, was not in love with her and did not wish to marry her, Lisa felt cornered to the point where, on Mother's Day, the previous Sunday, she had called Mother to ask her advice. Mother was shocked. Not so much at the reality, or even that this was a daughter she had raised within the Roman Catholic ethic, but that a thirty year old woman would call her mother for advice about such a thing, on Mother's Day, a bit over two weeks after her husband had died. In addition, Mother was staying at her sister's house. Mother had her own sense of propriety and pride. She would call Lisa back. She needed time to take in this appalling news. Suicide was not mentioned. The man had sent Lisa $500, the going rate in those days, for an illegal abortion.

I got this news Thursday evening, May 12th. I had neither pencil nor enough money with me to make the call, but I wet my finger and got Lisa's new phone number down on the dirty glass. Then I ran home to get money. I had already decided what I wanted to tell her: we had an extra room, quite separate from the house, and she and her baby were more than welcome to come and stay with us. The future would take care of itself. I wanted to assure her that I understood, I would never judge her, I would welcome her and her child, if that was what she wanted, into my life.

I was breathless when I got up the hill and to the back of the house where my husband was working. He agreed immediately to my plan, but cautioned me to wait on the phone call, that I was too excited and my alarm might convey itself to Lisa in a way that might be harmful. Somehow that made sense. I decided I'd call when I was calmer and could present the invitation in a way that would be acceptable. I would also speak more fully with Ellie on Saturday. Then I would call. I could barely sleep that night. I felt a terrible impatience to speak with Lisa, to let her know she was loved. I thought my heart would break for her. I did not know how soon and in how different a way that would happen.

Lisa brought Beethoven home. His Fifth Symphony.

Mother and Dad had taken us several times to hear a concert, just as they sometimes took us to the local museum of natural history. For Tommy and me, these visits, which required a certain seriousness as well as self-control, were not unlike being given medicine or an enema. So for Lisa to bring Beethoven into our home was astonishing.

Nor did she turn him on just once in a while; no, she had to listen several times a day. At first we exchanged glances to indicate our displeasure or ridicule, but that's as far as it went. With Lisa as his champion, Beethoven could not be stopped.

Lisa's unassailable reason for having him carry on two or three times a day was that she had to write a paper on him for her music appreciation class, this her freshman year in college. To write the paper, she had to understand him. And so he joined us beginning every afternoon when she returned from classes, his music filling every corner of our small house. There was no escape. It was too cold to go outdoors. We listened despite ourselves.

Beethoven flailed away even during dinnertime, replacing my father's news broadcast. The whole family vibrated with strings, horns, and percussion. He was obsessive, this Beethoven, with a passion that plunged far beneath the sentiment expressed in the 40's and 50's tunes we all loved. Oh, my father liked light classical music, and sometimes listened to the opera Saturdays on the radio, and I thought I knew something of serious music since I'd been studying ballet for three years. But all of this music had melody. Here was Beethoven with scarcely a tune banging away at something that couldn't be danced to by anything I had learned, that went beyond foot-tapping and physical reach.

I wouldn't say we liked him exactly, but after several days of this onslaught, one or another of us could be caught beating out the tempo, or humming along at a particularly delicate part, eyebrows raised expressively in accompaniment, and once, all of us formed a chorus of the four opening notes, followed by guilty laughter for our irreverance which Lisa indignantly hushed.

Mother was particularly delighted when she discovered that, put on at a high enough volume, Beethoven's opening phrases worked to awaken me in the mornings better than anything ever yet tried. I had always had difficulty reentering the everyday world, and my entry was soured by alarm clocks, my mother's persistent calls, or my sisters' proddings. But Beethoven banged on the door of my unconsciousness with the urgency of a neighbor at the door of a house on fire. His seriousness, matching that of the dream world I was so loathe to leave, created a bridge from that world to this and I arose, if not lively, at least thoughtful and alert.

But more than a week of the same symphony finally brought about a general protest. Tommy and I demanded equal time on the phonograph which had been moved up from the basement to the living room. I was teaching him be-bop and fox trot and Beethoven was hogging the show. Besides Lisa had written her paper.

Without my realizing, however, Beethoven touched something in me. I was fourteen years old; it would be several years more before my beliefs would come before the tribunal of my own conscience and awakening consciousness. But Beethoven alerted that consciousness. His music showed me there were other ways to explore depths that, until then, seemed to belong exclusively to religion. Here was a man who allowed something akin to God to sing through himself. I wasn't conscious of any of this, of course. But, as I listened first to him, then to Brahms, Schubert, and, later, Mozart, I saw how this business of God could not be so easily regulated into rituals and rules; that, in ways I could not understand let alone articulate, God belonged to these men, and if that was true, Mother Church had sprung a leak.

Because of Beethoven I chose Mr. Hart's music appreciation class as one of my electives. Slight of build, high-strung, sensitive, Mr. Hart wasn't cut out for high school teaching. His face revealed everything he felt and ought to have concealed, since his feelings vascillated between contempt for the lot of us and a quaking fear of the larger boys.

For openers, he asked if any of us could name a composer. The question was designed to make us look dumb. We all knew that, we'd been in school long enough. Silence, then:

"Glenn Miller."

Snorts.

"Patti Page, Frank Sinatra."

Open laughter.

"Beethoven," I called out. Mr. Hart located me among the voices, and stared. The class also turned to stare, smirks turning to annoyance. The last thing anyone wanted was a real lesson in music.

"Another one," he demanded.

I thought. "Kostelanetz."

"No, no, he's a conductor." But he was not only surprised, he was grateful. At the end of class, he stopped me.

"I get five or six free tickets every month for the concert series. No one takes them, so if you ever want one, just ask."

Involved in the school's annual variety show because of my dancing, I had gotten to know several of the 'brains' who made up the technical crew backstage. One was the brother of a close friend. He, my friend, Tommy, and three more of the crew decided we'd all go to that week's concert. I told Mr. Hart we needed seven tickets.

"Seven!" He covered his heart with one hand as he breathed the number. "Don't worry. I'll get them."

I adored theaters. Not only the stage and what occurred there, everything: from the rows of seats that faced the stage expectantly on the slight decline from back to front, to the immense velvet or satin curtains, silent sentinels between us and the magic until, with a great flourish, they were swept aside, or upward into ornate arches, as darkness fell with the accompanying hush when it was time at last for the dream to unravel. The theater was a pocket of reality where life, usually so much a muddle, or just humdrum, was made significant; it was a space in which my imagination and senses, emotions and intellect at last worked the way I'd been led to believe they ought to. Things turned out whether for good or for bad, and it was possible to know what had happened and why. I felt competent, fully human, in a theater.

Woolsey Hall lacked the curtains on the stage. Instead, gilded organ pipes rose up the back wall behind the empty seats where the orchestra sat. Otherwise, it had all the virtues of any other theater. But that first time, watching the orchestra members one by one take up their places, sometimes chatting with one another, then tuning up, was like watching someone take a bath publicly. I felt gypped in some way by the orchestra's unhidden preparation.

But to be in the concert hall meant I had to be there in precisely the same way the adults were: to listen, to be silent. No cutting up, no leaving halfway through with my friend, Joan, to check ourselves in the ladies' room mirror. The audience was as serious as Beethoven himself (though I came to see in later years that what I heard at fourteen was more a reflection of my own singleminded earnestness than Beethoven's). There I was, with my brother and friends, no parents, no older sisters, just us, in an audience filled with adults who paid us no attention, who talked and behaved with one another as if no youngsters were present. Here I felt grown up, released from the *isn't-she-cute-pat-on-the-head* syndrome that being the baby of the family entailed.

It didn't matter what the program was. To hear the music was to enter an architecture in which sound was the shaper, and the shaping consisted of emotion and idea instead of wood or plaster or stone. It didn't matter that I understood nothing of musical history or technique, even that I didn't know that the pause between movements did not signify the end, thus no applause, probably the most embarrassing moments for our little group until we grasped this convention, because the structure of music created a place for contemplating the universe in ways that were coherent to me. Sometimes the spaces I entered were familiar, but often they were so foreign that I could only allow understanding to settle viscerally, somewhere in my belly where it had to remain. This was how I knew lots of things, how I understood the world. It was why I danced, why I wanted to dance. Dance allowed me to express my understanding far beyond anything I comprehended intellectually.

But: I had to sit perfectly still. I wanted to dance, some part of me wanted to move, to find the precise gesture that went with what I imagined the composer was pointing to. And, clearly, this was forbidden. I didn't know how they did it, but everyone sat through even the most rhythmic pieces with not the hint of movement anywhere. They were like stone. Another blow for the body, the old separation of flesh and soul, flesh once again the loser. And so I forced myself to be still, to let the music move some inner dancer with her perfect, airy body. It didn't work. I discovered that people like myself, and there were others, sat way in the back where no one would notice this aberration, or be disturbed by it.

I didn't bother to pay attention to what was played by whom. I just wanted the freshness of experiencing whatever music was performed. But when I turned sixteen and got my first summer job, I joined a record club and started collecting my own recordings. Beethoven was joined by Tchaikovsky, Brahms, Schubert, all symphonic music, the only kind I knew, until Ellie's fiancé lent me a chamber piece by Mozart, and the musical world opened up in all its glory. Not everything had to be said in the large and often grand gestures of the symphony; the single voice of a clarinet or cello soared into realms of intimacy and tenderness I'd never dreamed might be allowed. In college, when at last I had a room of my own, I listened with the freedom that only solitude allowed me. I hummed along, directed the orchestra, danced, sometimes cried, breaking all the family taboos of expressing my emotions openly.

I moved on to other music, other composers, but Beethoven always held a special place in my heart. Wild, strange, at times melodramatic, especially in his long drawn-out endings, climax upon climax until I want to scream, "End, for God's sake, just end!" he was the one who opened the door into a realm that was the perfume hinted at in the incense used in church on special occasions. He taught me to have courage, demonstrating how deep a human voice could be, how far it could go, and thereby led me down the path I've followed ever since, a path without a name because it has no group, no consensus; it is only mine, though not mine alone. The Church was afraid of what Beethoven had to teach, afraid of its own saints whose ecstasy or suffering it liked to have captured in marble and colored glass where they would stay cool and safe and distant.

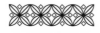

Reasons. Ah, to enter the safe little back yard of reasons. They are always at hand, lined up to offer themselves in various guises of attractiveness. *It was because of . . . She must have . . . .* To list circumstances and possibilities that would provide grounds for her act, or explain it, is to attempt to *encapsulate* her death in order to let it be swallowed up by apparent understanding. Swallowed, digested, and passed out into the world, her act then disapppears, evaporates, or gets filed under general headings to be trotted out at times to make a point. In either case, it *no longer matters.* And part of the point Lisa was making is that her act indeed mattered. Every suicide intends that in some way, even those whose choice makes more sense when faced with a long, painful dying. Most of us just get death, it comes, we dread it, ignore it, whatever. But we don't choose it. Lisa did. Therefore nothing can explain it, nothing digest it.

Besides, reasons only ever touch upon the surface of the inner landscape of suffering. Only a full experiencing of that territory might convey the how and why in ways that could let us feel it and understand it without dismissing it. Reasons are concocted afterwards, made up of a certain kind of thought and language, both linear in nature. Suffering is a totality.

Yet how tempting reasons are, how accustomed to them I am, how I only gave them up in Lisa's case because, even piled together, all those that I knew did not account for her choosing death. But as long as I clung to them, they led me into emotional deadends. I was angry—at her lack of courage, her self-pity, her striking out. I was afraid—we came from the same blood, the same background. And I was ashamed: suicide was the act of a defective, a deviant; in those days, no suicide was given the blessing of a Catholic burial. My own mother lied to everyone, hiding the truth in order to get her daughter the benefit of an afterlife. It was bad enough my father had just died; now my sister had killed herself. I hated the pity I felt directed at me from those who knew.

What reasons gave me were reactions. I never felt empathy for Lisa. I never expanded my heart beyond those puny reasons, my even punier reactions. How is it I was unable to imagine that Lisa suffered to such an extent that the thought of continuing life became unbearable? Would I have insisted that she live on despite such despair? Why? How can I measure her suffering, or her ability to handle it?

Death throws most of us into reverse gear under any circumstances, but suicide? All the platitudes we've learned fail here. The main thing we all want to know is "Why?" Everything else gets stuck on that. We drop our eyes, certain that the curiosity will show in them, mutter an "I'm so sorry," and make tracks out of the funeral parlor. But over the next few weeks we try to find out anything we can. And we hear things: "Her boyfriend broke up with her." It's a reason. We believe it, sure there must be more, but still it's a reason. It reassures in some way. Now Lisa is really dead. Gone, until some future time when someone mentions something, then, "Oh yes, I knew a young woman once who killed herself. Took pills. Boyfriend trouble or so I heard. Can you imagine killing yourself over some man?"

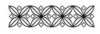

As if by magic, horses appeared in my life one summer evening. All of us were in the back yard, lazy around the picnic table where we'd had dinner of Mother's potato salad and meat loaf, Dad's corn and string beans fresh from the garden he tended with a mixture of love and irritation. Ellie, Lisa and Mother began gathering up the dishes. Dad, Tommy and I settled in beach chairs as we so often did summer nights in the hopes of a breeze starting up and just to be surrounded by the falling night. It was just before dusk, the trees turning black against the sky, the frogs down in the woods tuning up for their evening concert. Suddenly I heard a sound I had only ever heard in movies: hoofbeats. Tommy and I ran to the back hedge. Two riders on magnificent horses passed. We gaped. Both riders and horses looked sideways at us. No one said anything.

The dirt road bordering the back yard was a fresh scar cut through the pines by the water company to lay in a sewer line for the post-war developments springing up around us; it ended about a mile up from our house. So they had to come back. We stationed ourselves now on the woods side of our hedge, inventing openings to conversations that would allow us to truly take in this miracle. And here they came at a gallop.

"Hi!" we called out. "Hi!"

They smiled and waved. And kept on going.

But the next time they appeared, several weeks later, after many evenings of fruitlessly watching and listening, we ran to greet them, and flagged them down. I was too frightened of the horses to approach—this close, they were immense—but the couple understood our longing and walked them up to where we stood on the embankment, and I looked into the eyes of one. I was smitten; forever it seems, convinced even to this day that there is something I must learn from these animals, without any notion of what that might be. Mystery perhaps, my own mystery, the same as that of all existence, which the huge silence of a horse so fully embodies.

Three years before, I had pleaded and wheedled for dance lessons, now I begged for the two dollars it cost to ride for an hour. With my brother a partner in this, Mother and Dad caved in.

I don't know what Tommy's motives were; mine were connected to that sense of mystery, as well as to dance. Dance without practice since it was the horse who did the moving. And dance as the beauty I could not fulfill myself but which existed as a thirst that needed this water. And so up we went onto the backs of strange beasts, surely with terror, but with that insouciance toward risk that accompanies ignorance. And mostly there was no real danger. We rode stable horses: tired, bedraggled creatures resigned to their sad lives ruled by riders like ourselves who understood nothing of their desire to fulfill their innate grace.

I began drawing horses obsessively. I read every horse story and novel I could find. I rode as often as I could afford to all through high school. In college, I was able to take riding lessons for one credit of my gym requirements, and learned the mechanics of English saddle riding. Not one of the horses I rode had the nobility I drew, read about, and yearned for.

Had I practiced and continued with dance, I might have achieved something. Certainly I loved it and felt the music sweep through me so that every muscle knew intuitively what it was supposed to do, how it should lift, leap, or fly.

But what I felt in my body and what I saw in the mirror did not coincide. I was eleven when I started. I did not know about patience or development. Mother encouraged me in tap which required nothing more than rhythm, a certain syncopated fluidity. I was after beauty, grace, expression. Tap was fun, ballet a transformation.

I studied for three years. I improved, sometimes even looked good, but I was not satisfied. I quit, returning again in my senior year in high school for another two years so that dance and riding once again conjoined. Riding won out, especially when I met Misty D.

A friend discovered a stable, way out in the countryside, unlike any I'd ever gone to. It was owned and operated by a man who clearly loved his animals. Kind and talkative, he would not let anyone run his horses the way other public stables did. Nor did he hire the usual toughs I'd seen at every other stable, hard men with at least one or two teeth missing, whose advice to us novice riders was always to kick or yell or pull on the reins. The occasional help he did hire never got to do anything concerning the horses other than shovelling up or pitching hay. Mr. O'Connor did everything else, his wife helping when the work was too much for him.

That first time, when I asked for an English saddle-trained horse, Mr. O'Connor looked at me appraisingly.

"Well, I do have one maybe you can try. But only in the ring. Wait here. I'll get her ready."

He disappeared into the dark mouth of the barn. My friend and I sat on the grass in the shade of a huge elm.

It was quiet. The country road was behind us; occasionally a car sped past. Otherwise we heard only the steady rippling of the stream that cut through the close-cropped fields surrounding the barn. It was mid-morning and hot. Not even birds were stirring. The trees across the fields appeared weighted in the humid, breezeless, air. But the humidity intensified the odors of horse and hay, odors I loved, as much as I loved the peculiar smell of freshly sewn costumes of fake satin and sequins that we wore once a year for our recital at the Schubert Theater in downtown New Haven. For me, that would always be the smell of backstage, with the thrill and terror and exhilaration associated with the theater.

The first I saw of Misty D was the white flame that flared up her nose to just under her forelock as she stood inside the darkness of the barn. I watched, unbelieving, as she emerged, her whole body dancing with an anticipation just barely held in check by her consent to submit. Other than that single flash of white, she was uniformly a deep chestnut, her mane and tail black. Seventeen hands tall, she was probably part thoroughbred, but I never learned what she was, or cared. Everything she was was perfectly evident: spirited, vain, proud, elegant, sensitive and intelligent. She was precisely what I wanted to be.

As I approached her, I saw that it was not only Mr. O'Connor by whom I was being measured. She snorted and threw her head, then arched herself gracefully as I lifted my leg to mount. Mr. O'Connor led her to the ring himself. Only when we were inside did he allow me the reins.

Misty D danced to the center, her head turned slightly so she could continue to take me in. I signalled her with both hands and leg to move out to the rail, did it twice, before I realized she was already on her way.

I hadn't expected such cooperation, nor the thrill that came with it. To work in concert with a creature as large and powerful as a horse is to experience one's own body as an intelligence. And to work with one who has chosen to work with you is to experience an honest humility. Force, with bits and whips and spurs, does not get a horse to move in the way Misty D moved.

Force breaks a horse; she moves because she has to, but without energy, without style.

It was owing to my gentleness and caring rather than to any ability or experience that Mr. O'Connor, who watched me ride the full hour, told me at the end, "Well, you can come out here any time you want and ride her. For free," he added with a big grin when I reacted with dumbfounded amazement. "She needs the workout. But only in the ring. I don't want her taking off on you out in those woods."

I knew little, so I still thought that I was in charge, I was the teacher. In spite of me, Misty D taught me her dance, one she had worked for harder than I had ever worked, and which she did with such patience and enthusiasm, one could only surmise it was done from joy. She never balked. On the contrary, I could tell if anyone was watching us work, even from a distance, because her body became even more electric. She would flex her neck, throw up her tail, and kick out, not so much in a buck as in a capriole.

"Show off," Mr. O'Connor laughed the first time she did it and I got scared. He watched the two of us with pride. "Maybe you'll get to ride her in the county show next year, you keep practicing like that."

Because of my training in dance, I knew something I might not have otherwise: I could follow, I could feel the rhythm Misty D established and go with it. Oh, I pretended, as she did, that my kicks and prods and pulls were the stuff of a real horse-woman, but I know better now. I was on the back of a great artist who was not about to let me ruin her stuff. She suffered me perhaps because she was fine enough to recognize I was in awe of her.

No one in my family ever saw me on Misty D. For one thing, I had to get up and leave early in order to get to the stable before the most stifling heat of the day set in. But mainly, no one was really interested. Horses were animals. They stank. They were physical the way animals always are physical. Sometimes embarrassingly so.

I never grasped the necessity for the concept underlying the separation of body and soul, and certainly never accepted it as the truth it pretended to be. I believed with great certainty that I knew better. Connected to this first heresy was my refusal to accept hierarchies, a belief that would ultimately lead to my own equality with God. But that would come much later. As a girl, I kept things centered around what was important to me. Animals, bodies of every sort—trees, rocks, plants, buildings, clouds, mountains, snowflakes—were one with spirit and no one could convince me otherwise.

Thus I was flabbergasted around fourth grade when the nun in our Tuesday afternoon catechism classes said that animals did not go to Heaven. I was sure she must be joking. But when I asked Father Daley about it, he affirmed the statement in the strongest terms. As did Mother. Only Dad, not Catholic, but sworn to silence on such subjects until we kids should grow to the age of reason, kept his silence but with a particular smile, the barest hint that perhaps I knew what I knew and should trust that thoroughly.

And so I secretly clung to my own view, sure Father Daley must simply be mistaken, the only way I could maintain a precarious balance with the Church and my own independence of thought. I knew nothing of heresy, not even the word, but I certainly understood that I was to accept the priest's word as the truth.

But what sort of God would it be to allow animals to lapse into nothing? Certainly Tootsie, our neighbor's cat, with her fierce eyes and untamable temper, was not merely making a temporary appearance, all that fury for nothing. Or Pepper, the little brown mutt who ran the neighborhood dog world with efficiency and good humor, but at whose silent stare, the largest dog would freeze or quickly slink away.

If dance and horses taught me anything, it was the union of body and spirit, the oneness and wholeness of my self.

In the late autumn a bolt of lightning hit Mr. O'Connor's barn. It burned to the ground. Only one horse survived, a mustang that had been captured in the wild. Mr. O'Connor said he came running out of the barn, nose to the ground, his back aflame. They caught him and got the fire out. For months, his scarred back was greasy with salve. No one knew how he got free of his rope.

Misty D had to be shot along with a dozen other horses. Unlike the mustang, she had no experience in survival. She kept rearing, throwing her head high, sucking in the smoke so her lungs were ruined. I couldn't understand why Mr. O'Connor didn't choose to just put her out to pasture as he did the mustang, but probably he couldn't bear it. Nor could Misty D. She was no longer simply a horse. She was a performer, a dancer. However it happened, she had joined us humans in our particular experiment. She thrived on the show, on meeting the challenges this other species asked of her.

"You move like a dancer," a young woman would tell me years later when dance and horses were far removed from my life. Her words lit me up in a way that turned an observation into a compliment. It was as if she had seen into a central core, one I myself had forgotten about amidst marriage, child-rearing, teaching and troubles.

I moved like a dancer, which, to me, meant I moved with grace, a sense of body within space, conversant with the physical objects around me. My body expressed me: I moved like a dancer, like a horse, a planet in rhythm with the universe.

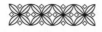

I had learned it was possible to live without emotional pain. I was learning this long before Lisa's suicide, not just to live without pain, but without feeling itself. It was one of the more serious lessons of my childhood. I misunderstood an important aspect of the real lesson: emotions themselves were not terrible, only the expression of them, particularly in public. But young and both emotional and expressive, I failed to catch that subtle difference. Confusing the two, I began to shut down at the source. Oddly, emotions became bigger, even more frightening, capable of taking me over. The more they insisted, the harder I struggled with their control.

To dull pain requires a general dulling. This is obvious in hindsight, not so visible as one gradually develops the skills: keeping busy; making light of perfectly serious matters; allowing few people to know anything that's happened, let alone how you feel; and when someone begins to express sympathy, change the subject, divert. Move on. Never suggest a serious subject, or do so only in an offhand manner. Guarded this way from others, one begins to be guarded as well from oneself.

Such protection comes at a cost. The dulling spreads to other areas. Even in my twenties, I noticed a lessened response to things I loved deeply: music, theater, dance, literature, even nature. I took refuge in animals, our various dogs and cats. They were all I felt safe with. Emotionally I was committing a kind of living suicide.

My body recognized the crime for what it was and tried to do the feeling for me. When I visited my father as he lay dying, I underwent an event in which I simulated his condition. I was overwhelmed first by diarrhea, this within a day or so of having seen his bedpan filled with bloody urine. Then my throat closed on me and

I lay gasping, certain in my semi-lucid state that I had been poisoned. My lucidity was limited to an acute self-observation; to Mother and a frantic Ellie, I was otherwise oblivious, unable to pull my consciousness away from what was happening within my body.

During the next six weeks until my father died, I suffered an itching so severe I was covered with scabs from having scratched myself in my sleep. Reality piled one disaster upon the other: Lisa killed herself three weeks after Dad's death; Mother was stunned by this additional grief; Tommy was shipped off to Vietnam; and my marriage was in its final throes; I was facing a future alone with my four year old daughter. Suddenly, about a week before I was going to announce my separation to my spouse, I suffered two grand mal seizures.

Is it simplistic to connect the seizures to my suppressed emotions? I do not see the body as an entity discrete from either the mind or spirit. I believe there has to be a conversation between them, a kind of balancing act. Emotion is one of the bridges between body and spirit; when it gets clogged, something's going to break down.

Due to my mistaken understanding, I learned that the denial of feelings was a sign of strength. It is not. Strength consists in telling oneself the truth. If suffering is the result of the truth, then so it is. It is the result in any case, but with truth, suffering passes through like the season it is. With denial, the winds just keep blowing, the winter goes on and on. My personal winter is just now ending. It has been twenty five years long.

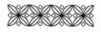

In the spring of my third year of college, after weeks of agonizing, I told my parents I wanted to quit school when the semester ended. I tried to convey my despair, which was real and serious, a despair I hoped would dissipate once I got out into what I imagined to be a different, and real, world. They let me know, as they never had before, the extent to which they had sacrificed to put the four of us through college. I was the last, and I had only one more year. I honestly didn't see how I could go through another academic year—I wasn't doing that well, I was deeply depressed—but promised I'd take the summer to think it over.

My problem was love. The year before I'd fallen in love for the first time. All previous attractions had been schoolgirl crushes that quickly fizzled when I got to know the real boy. But this one lasted, deepened even, in the long, intense conversations we had at the back tables of the town's college hangouts where the tepid tea I drank enhanced my romance not only with him but with the nihilism he espoused.

He was Jewish; I was still very much an ardent Catholic. This didn't have to be a problem, I believed, but he let me know that his parents would have buried an empty coffin, metaphor for his symbolic death, if he ever married me. That was probably not true, they weren't religious Jews. More likely, the idea of marriage, toward which I was by then most definitely moving, was not what he wanted, but his announcement of this awakened me to the fact that this love had no future. To me, love without a future was sordid. Choices in the '50's were quite clear, though perhaps less repressed women escaped the black and white nature of female virtue. I wasn't one of these, however, so the only choice I could make was to end the relationship. I did, the summer before my third year of college. This was the source of my anguish.

In the last weeks of May of that year, during finals, the hardest time of the academic year under the best of circumstances, I got a mysterious call from Lisa. Could she come to the dorm to talk to me? Her voice conveyed the promise of something. I waited the half hour it would take her to drive from home to the college, glad to have an excuse to quit studying for my next exam.

She joined me in the basement smoker, saying nothing until the other women left. Her eyes danced with excitement then as she turned to me. "How would you like to go to Finland with me?"

I didn't understand.

She stubbed out her cigarette and sat on the edge of the rickety chair. "The company that has hired me has a sister company further north, in Rovaniemi, on the Arctic Circle, about four hours away from where I'll be, and they want an American teacher up there too. Do you want to go?"

"When? When would we go?"

"In September, for a year. Nine months in Finland, and a couple of months travelling in Europe."

I almost wept. I was Cinderella at the stroke of midnight. "How can I? I have my senior year. Mom and Dad . . . ."

She interrupted. "It's all taken care of. Mom and Dad want you to go. They've already talked to the dean, and if you say yes, she's approved a year's leave of absence. When you come back, you finish your senior year."

There have been a few times since then when something has happened that has conveyed that same sense of deliverance.

I leaped from my chair and whooped. Lisa and I embraced, laughed.

"Girls!" we heard a stern voice call from the top of the stairs. It was Miss Lucy, the housemother. I ran to the staircase and looked up at her.

"I'm sorry," I whispered. "I forgot." I was beaming. "I just got some great news."

Miss Lucy grimaced, the closest she ever came to a smile.

"I'm going to Europe," I said, only half-believing it myself. "I'm going to Europe."

"That's wonderful, my dear, but you must observe quiet hours during exams."

I nodded and raced back to Lisa.

"You haven't heard the best part yet."

What could be better? I was getting out of school for a year. I was having a dream come true, the dream of travelling to cities and countries, places I'd never thought I'd ever get to. I could hardly stand still.

"Mom and Dad are paying our way on . . ." She paused for effect.

"What, what?" I prodded.

"The Queen Elizabeth!"

We both leaped and danced and whooped some more. But quietly. I did not want to be grounded these last few days of school.

My bags were packed and ready by the end of June and, other than my waitress uniforms that I used on my summer job, I had only one pair of jeans and a few tops left to wear. It didn't matter. I wasn't going anywhere. Every week, I carefully unpacked and repacked, adding things now and then as I made extra money. I saved as much as I could. Once there, I would get a room and small salary, but I didn't know how far that would go.

Lisa bought a Finnish language record and we practiced when we could. I was utterly mystified however. Having studied and done well in French, German and Latin, I could not even begin to master the intricacies Finnish presented. I practiced the first three lessons over and over, then decided I'd just pick the language up once I got there. I figured it would be easy.

I was twenty years old. I came from a background that taught me the necessity of work, the value of education, though on this latter one, I was ready to pull the plug. It was a background that never promised the possibility of what now awaited me. I assumed only the rich went to Europe, but here I now stood, with Lisa, my parents, and a few friends, on the deck of one of the most glamorous ships to sail the sea. All of us were enchanted, Lisa and I to such an extent we made no effort to hide our excitement. Like kids, we went from ballroom to lounge to dining room. Our stateroom, way below deck, and crowded with two other travellers, thrilled us with its economical use of space.

Standing on the upper deck in the bright September sun as the ship blasted its deep-throated signal for departure, then shivered heavily, churning up the river as it pulled away from the dock, my parents and friends waving, all of us smiling, laughing, crying, as they first, then the skyscrapers of New York, got smaller and smaller, was for me like entering into a living fairy tale. Lisa beside me was the magical godmother who had somehow made all this come true.

The magic lasted for the five days it took to cross the Atlantic. We found our way through the labyrinths of the huge ship and made forbidden jaunts over to first and second class where the opulence astounded and delighted us. Even in our class—tourist, the cheapest—everything was more than we could have wished for. All meals were served on china, with silver gleaming against white linen. We had high tea every day at four on the dot, danced every evening, strolled the decks or stood in the bow to watch the sea trail like a comet behind us.

We spent three days in England where I, an English major, shivered in awe at just about everything. Most moving, however, was the moment I stood beside Chaucer's tomb in Westminster Abbey. I had just spent the last semester reading almost all of his *Canterbury Tales* and all of *Troilus and Criseide*, so I was filled with the lilt and rhythm of his English, his wit and depth and humor. And now here he was, here his bones were, behind the grey stones of the wall. Lisa grinned when she saw the tears in my eyes.

We went to Stratford-on-Avon to Shakespeare's house and gardens, and walked the path he himself had walked through the wildflower-filled fields to Anne Hathaway's cottage. We were the perfect age, the perfect companions, Lisa and I, with the same level of energy, the same thrill of innocence that lit up everything and everyone with a bright glow. For once, I awakened early without difficulty. We took in people, buildings, events, with an unappeasable appetite.

When we finally arrived in Helsinki, at night, by train, we felt for the first time the reality of what we were getting into. It happened via the language. One of the phrases we had learned was "Where is a restaurant?" —a phrase we needed at that particular point since nothing resembling a restaurant was anywhere in view.

"*Missa on ravintola?*" first she, then I, tentatively asked a couple of pedestrians. Whatever they said, it was not one of the phrases we'd learned on our record. Their hands and arms told us more. Lugging our suitcases, we walked for blocks until we found a dreary, poorly-lit *ravintola* filled only with men who stared at us throughout our meal.

But the greater reality set in the next day as we said our farewells when Lisa disembarked from the plane that took us north. I continued on to Rovaniemi, alone, among people who were clearly pleasant to me, but whose language I could make no sense of. When the plane landed in the darkness, I looked for the company's representative who was supposed to meet me. People passed me by and left the small, emptying airport; I looked around with greater anxiety. I had just begun to wonder what I was going to do when a man speaking a very peculiar English made it clear he was the company's representative come to pick me up. I got into his car and was whisked off into the tall, piney night.

The Rovaniemi I had pictured was a dark, primitive village out of another century, the people and life Dostoevskian in all ways. The real Rovaniemi was a clean, bright, definitely twentieth century town with people whose resemblance to Dostoevsky began and ended with their Russian fur caps, necessary against the unbelievable cold that set in in early October and remained relentlessly until the end of April.

I moved in with the Kuorikoski family rather than live on my own in a furnished efficiency, as Lisa chose to do. The couple, Elja and Hannele, had two daughters, Sinnika, aged six, and Kikka, nine, and a Rottweiler named Anu. I was given the large upstairs bedroom in their comfortable and very contemporary home and was free to use the kitchen as I wished. About a month after I arrived, Elja left for a six month stay in the United States. As a result, Hannele and I became fast friends with the kind of freedom single roommates have, long afternoons and evenings to discuss the world, explore our differences. Hannele was, needless to say, fluent in English, as my Finnish never progressed beyond the barest necessities except for one flourish: my ability to talk about the weather. There I was fairly proficient, especially about cold and snow.

My teaching consisted of hour-long lessons with employees, mostly one-on-one, with an occasional small group lesson. I was a disaster. I have no idea now why, but I never did anything to prepare myself for this work. I suppose I figured since I'd been a student all my life, not to mention a brief stint of teaching English to refugees from Hungary in 1956, that I just *knew* how it was done. I didn't, and the feeling of failure gradually crept in. The beginning level students quietly dropped away; the intermediate learners did too, except for a couple of really determined ones. Even my very advanced students started skipping their lessons (a euphemism at best) toward the end of my stay. I'm amazed they hung in there as long as they did. Politeness no doubt. The Finns are very polite.

But the teaching had never been my reason for going to Finland. I was on an adventure, like Alice, there to observe and absorb, and this I did with great success. Several of my students befriended me and took me off on excursions, like berry picking in the tundra; others taught me how to cross-country ski, and took me to the lodge at the top of Ounasvaara, the soft Arctic fell that overlooked the town. I was invited on Saturday nights to go dancing at Pohjanhovi, the town's swankiest hotel where European bands played tangos and waltzes, and stiff young men approached our table to request a dance from one of us. We'd dance, saying nothing, and at its end, bow slightly with a "*Kiitos,*" then be escorted back to the table until the next one approached. I drank wine and smoked openly, behavior that scandalized everyone, as women did neither publicly. I enjoyed the notoriety, particularly when I discovered that the reason the women went off to the ladies room so often was to take a swig or two from the flasks they kept hidden in their purses, and to puff away on the harsh Finnish cigarettes.

I walked the town on my own day or night—and by December it was night all the time—with nothing to fear but the nasty little dogs that inhabited every house on every residential street, and even they only barked, albeit with a snarling enthusiasm. During my first month, Hannele had told me about the rape and murder of two young women camping up north in the tundra. It was a horrible story, especially because the crime was never solved, but when she said it had happened three years before I was astonished. In America, even back in the '50's, no one bothered to'talk about an incident that old. Murder and rape that got discussed were no less than a couple of months old. I didn't worry about my safety after that.

I discovered the library with its small but adequate English section. I quickly devoured just about everything I wanted to read. This was heaven. For the first time, I was pursuing an education in the way I believed it should be pursued, with time to savor what I was reading without the pressure of papers, exams, or grades. I discussed everything I read or noticed with Hannele whose quick mind and wit always brought in something new, something I hadn't thought of. Her kitchen where we sat over tea and coffee was the best classroom I ever had.

Without Hannele, her daughters, the dog, and later, when he returned, Elja, the loneliness and homesickness that periodically overcame me might have been permanent companions. I sometimes walked the streets looking up at the clouds that stretched westward back toward home and wished I could swing up onto one of them and sail back to where everyone could speak my tongue, to where I understood what was going on without puzzlement, where I felt immediately understood by those around me. I learned during those nine months in Rovaniemi how very American I was, something I would not have believed to be true let alone attractive before my sojourn there. I'd always

liked having a cosmopolitan image of myself. I belonged anywhere, had the Ingrid Bergmanesque *savoir-faire* to be free of
boundaries and culture, and certainly the low-brow culture I
believed America represented. But not now. I longed for low-
brow, longed for the flat, twangy Americanese I'd always es-
chewed, longed for rock and roll, for Coke, fresh salads, pizza,
even television.

These spells would come over me for days at a time. On
Thursday mornings, I had to take the company van that drove
me a couple of hours out to one of the power stations where I
gave lessons to the engineers and their wives on Thursday afternoon, Friday, and Saturday morning; after that, I was returned to
Rovaniemi, and was free then until Monday morning. When I
was there, I was really alone and spent most of my time, outside
the hours of lessons, reading or writing in my room in the
company's guest house.

I took *sauna* on Friday night, alone. The first time I took
it I hadn't the slightest idea how it was supposed to work. I
undressed and went in to the hot room and sat on the lowest
bench. I'd been told only that it was supposed to be quite hot and
that, after sweating, one was supposed to rush out into the snow
and roll around. I wasn't about to rush out anywhere. It was forty
degrees below zero. But I began to throw more water on the hot
stones. My throat burned with a dry heat each time I did, but the
room didn't seem to get any hotter. After a while, I climbed up to
the top bench. I fell forward, my head between my knees, gasping
for air. I was suddenly perspiring profusely, the apparent goal for
taking *sauna*, so I grabbed my soap and began to lather my sweaty
body, with a certain distaste at soaping up in my own perspira-
tion. I then went into the next room and showered in coldish
water, the closest I would come to the snow business. I'd forgotten a towel, so had to return to the hot room to dry off enough to
put on my clothes. By the time I walked the sixty or so feet back
to the guesthouse, my wet hair was frozen solid. Hannele ex-

plained that weekend, through gales of laughter, the niceties of the *sauna*. One does not wash in one's own sweat, I learned.

I also learned that the escape I thought could be achieved by changing environments was an illusion. No matter that I was in a strange land, thousands of miles from home and those back rooms of coffee shops. No matter that each day was new and different. I was the same person who'd moped through the previous year. I moped less, but I was still bewildered by the loss of something I could not replace or forget, hurt by a reality that denied me something I so deeply wanted. It was a real disappointment to have the same familiar me awaken each morning.

Lisa and I took turns visiting each other about once a month. For her, especially, so much on her own, it was a relief to be able to talk naturally. She was far superior to me as a teacher — she had taken the work seriously from the start—as well as a student of Finnish. But she developed some quirks over that year, perhaps from an abundance of loneliness. She seemed determined to be the perfect American abroad, and her normal politeness and sensitivity to others became stilted, unnatural. And during the Christmas holiday, when we visited Ellie and her husband who were spending a year in southern Germany, Ellie and I became alarmed once when she said something totally out of context to the conversation we had been having. I don't recall what she said, only its effect: Ellie, her husband and I just gaped at her, then at each other. She seemed to be talking out of some distant and private place, completely disconnected from the three of us. But it was only a moment. After that, though we watched and listened, no such thing reoccurred.

One of my students was an elderly man, probably in his sixties, but with the bearing and pride of a much younger man, still very manly and attractive. It became clear by our fifth or sixth lesson that he was developing a romantic interest in me. I was flattered, but embarrassed, and hadn't the slightest idea how to discourage him. Besides being old enough to be my grandfather, he was married. Hannele was sure I was mistaken so didn't offer any solid suggestions. She was more amused by it than anything. One lesson, he brought what no doubt was passionate love poetry and read it aloud to me—in Finnish—taking up half of the hour with an impenetrable garble of words, lovingly rolling his r's, caressing the vowels of his beloved native tongue which sounded to me, however, like rounds from a machine gun. I bit my lip to keep from laughing as he went on and on probably saying things that would have brought the blood rushing to my face had I understood. And should have made him blush as well. Again, Hannele just laughed. But weeks later, when he grabbed me at the elevator door as we were leaving the building, and, as they say in romantic novels, crushed me against his chest, and forced me to kiss him, she advised me to tell him to, as we say in American, knock it off. I did, as politely as I could, and he ceased his amorous attentions.

A month later, at the company Christmas party, he asked me to dance with him. The whole company was there, there was no danger. We stepped onto the floor as the band began to play a waltz. We started tentatively, then gathered momentum as each understood the other's possibilities. Soon we were soaring. We waltzed together as though we had practiced for this moment all of our lives. People stood aside to watch as we went from one end of the floor to the other. He held my eyes, and, young as I was, what I saw in them was what I had chosen to miss. He was a prince, his grace and elegance equally apparent in the dance and in his gentlemanly acceptance of loss. He showed me that and then disappeared from my life, never again appearing for lessons. After that I only saw him at a distance. I should have learned from him, but I've never taken losses well.

Death is the most peculiar, most mysterious, part of being alive. That we cease to exist in the way we experience ourselves now—through our senses, within space and the dailiness of time, with the blue sky, the rainy day, amid all of our thoughts, ideas and feelings—is the most fascinating puzzle—beyond comprehension. It doesn't even matter whether we believe in an afterlife or in nothing at all; that we are here now, this way, and then not here, remains astonishing despite all human explanations or personal beliefs. Nothing alters the absolute fact of death. Death calls all of life into question: its meaning, whether it even has meaning, ethics, morality, every human institution, all of our future and our past.

Suicide does all this and more. It is like death's personal calling card dropped off at the doors of the survivors. It alerts us, and alarms us, because the suicide has dived directly into the mystery itself. I'm not talking now about the guilt we feel for not having noticed the pain, for not doing something, making that call, not any of that. I'm talking about the ontological chill that runs through us. Suicide brings death about as close as it can get; we can't help but recognize how close its border really is, how thin the membrane between us and it. With my father's death, I could take particular stances: he was ill, it was a relief that his pain was ended, his death was part of a natural process. None of this applied to Lisa. With her death, I cracked like an egg. She touched me with the mystery itself.

Suicide represents the ultimate in individualism, and, in Christian tradition, has long been considered the worst, the arch sin. Even murder is not so bad. To choose to die is to slap God in the face because suicide implies that life is not valuable, and life, presumably, is God's gift. Today our society is beginning to consider suicide as a possibility for people who are terminally ill. To consider this means we must examine the value of life itself, whether just being alive is in itself a worthy thing. Lisa made that examination within herself, as has every suicide like her. She—they—decided it wasn't. Perhaps only that single soul can make such a decision. The rest of us are left to live with it.

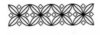

The Arctic tundra is one of the few places on earth where it is possible to hear absolute silence. I mentioned this to our ski instructor.

"Oh, would you like to hear?" He was our age, very attractive.

"Oh yes. Please." Lisa's response rang with the overenthusiasm of a teacher. Her smile matched. It was my idea in the first place and now, having seen how pleased Yuri was, she was acting as though it were hers. Like most Europeans, Finns had expectations about Americans. That we should want something so deep and simple as silence was not typical. He was impressed.

We skiied away from the lodge, over the fells that rose up out of the vast snowy land the way waves rise in the immensity of the sea. Gentle, rounded hills, they were marked at their bases by rock outcroppings and skimpy lines of low brush. Here and there a pine would rise up, no more than fifteen or twenty feet high, to break the flatness of the horizon. But these too had a thinness about them, as though deprived of air or soil. Here were not the unending forests of tall, reaching pines that covered the rest of Finland. This was a land where everything was pared down to all it could be and still exist; this was what survival looked like.

Lisa and I would be here a week, everything paid for by our employers. The lodge we stayed in encompassed the Finnish worlds of old and new. The old part was built of thick logs, hand-hewn and polished to a high gloss. Long contemporary windows had been more recently cut in the two sides that did not contain the fireplace with its open hearth surrounded by a full wall of stone. The windows overlooked the barren tundra into which we now ventured and which seemed to inspire the austere and practical aspect of the lodge's new wing. This part, by far the larger, contained the eight long dormitory rooms with double bunk beds and Spartan furnishings. It also contained a gleaming white kitchen that stood open to a new chrome and polished pine dining room with buffet tables filled three times a day with Finnish delicacies: smoked reindeer meat, pickled herring with beets and potatoes, hot cereals seasoned with dried fruits, pancakes with strawberry preserves, sweet stuffed cabbage, and breads of all shapes and flavors spanning the sweet to sour spectrum, accompanied by pyramids of balls of butter patterned by the decorative wooden spatulas used to roll them. The windows in the old part had once been small against the fierce cold until the modern capacity for triple-glazing spawned the new Finnish architecture with its preference for openness, light, and simplicity, a union of grace and function which appealed to me once I gave up my preconceived desire for an old and dark, almost medieval, culture. Other than old farms with their rickety wooden animal pens, nearly everything in Finland was new. There was a brilliance in design, an exuberance in chrome and steel and glass tempered to a human warmth. Every coffeehouse, waiting room, office building, contained that brilliance; every Finnish home I entered combined the cold with the warm with an unerring feel for comfort and welcome.

"There is no life here," Yuri said, meaning during the winter. "No birds, no animals. Nothing to make a noise except for the wind."

"Yes, and today is perfectly still." Again the enthusiastic note.

"Aren't any birds back yet?" I asked.

"No. It is too early."

It was mid-April, and though the sun was strong enough for us to feel its warmth so long as we kept moving, the land was stiff and frozen as far as we could see.

Yuri stepped to one side of the ski trail in order to observe us.

"Glide," he said to me, establishing a rhythm. "Glide, pole, glide. There, that's better."

He pushed ahead to watch Lisa. "Yes, good, very good." He smiled at her and returned to the lead position.

We stopped at the base of a fairly large fell.

"There," he said, pointing to the top, "we shall listen to the silence."

I felt an excitement I could not explain. I was unaware of how important silence was to me. I had lived within its myriad forms—in church, by the river, afternoons beneath the apple trees, in so many places, in so many seasons, but always accompanied by sound: the church organ, voices in the distance, or the single call of a phoebe or crow or jay—and not known what it was I was listening for. Silence pointed to the sacred, the sacred being the human capacity for awe and wonder; it was itself a sacred presence, the headwaters for language, song, laughter, dance. Here, at the top of the world, I was about to hear it as a physical reality.

Near the top, Yuri stopped.

"Here?" I asked. He nodded.

I listened. We were all breathing hard.

"Shhh. Let's try to hold our breath, just for a minute."

How do you hear silence? There was no wind. There were no birds, there was no sound and yet there was the sound one hears at night in a quiet room, a soft, yet persistent, whoosh, the sound of the inside of one's own ears, or brain, but something. I was profoundly disappointed. I had wanted the sound of nothing at all, no sound, and there apparently was no such thing. I was annoyed when Lisa laughed softly and said, "How wonderful," as if we had actually heard it. She had said it for Yuri, nothing else.

The Finns only rarely spoke to foreigners out of their heritage, things they themselves held in common as knowledge, but which might appear primitive or silly to outsiders. One of the things a few had mentioned was "Lapland fever", a condition Lisa and I would giggle about, as if it were an impossibility to fall under the spell of a wasteland. But here in the midst of the tundra, I was struck by its vastness broken only by this softest whoosh inside my own ears. Lisa and I would still laugh about it later, but, after this, I knew it was something that could happen. My laughter would come out of nervousness rather than derision. The last thing I wanted was to fall under its spell.

We cut across the slope as we headed down. This was my favorite part—I was flying.

"Knees!" Yuri yelled. "Bend your knees."

It was too late. The tops of my skis caught the hole before I even saw it. I went sailing, landed, face first in the soft snow.

"Are you all right?" Yuri's voice was just above me. My sunglasses were askew, my face and hair covered with snow. One of my skis was stuck behind me, tip down, keeping me pinned, the other I saw gliding sideways down the slope, gathering momentum as it went.

Yuri extracted me from the one ski and I managed to stand up, attempting to hide my embarrassment by vigorously brushing the snow off.

Lisa's voice was ripe with concern. "Are you okay?"

In our family, laughter was a bond, a comforting embrace, particularly at embarrassing or humiliating moments. Once, when the heel of Mother's shoe broke, and she ended up wrapped around a tree, what saved her was the four of us kids up on the sidewalk above her, slapping our thighs, eyes streaming with tears, bent over with the pain of laughter. Oh, we helped her up with the assistance of some other churchgoers, and though she would herself tell this story with a pretended horror at her children's callous behavior, every one of us knew it was the only behavior that prevented total humiliation, her there, draped around a tree in her best fox collar winter coat, her new pillbox hat with its delicate veil halfway down her face, real pearl earrings, and kid skin gloves. In that precise moment, she knew she had raised us right. So that Lisa wasn't laughing at my fall indicated the seriousness of this business of Yuri, who was on his way to collect my errant ski. Lisa and I had never been competitive before in relation to men; our difference in age had precluded that. I saw she would be as relentless in this pursuit as she was with all her goals. She would not give way to me, nor would I be easily forgiven if in fact I won. Yuri was not worth it; at most he was a week's flirtation. I started to laugh. She joined in, halfheartedly at first, then with the full embrace I so badly needed.

As it turned out, Yuri wasn't winnable anyway. His girlfriend arrived that night, moved in with three other young women into the dormitory room Lisa and I had had to ourselves for two days. Lisa and I were enthusiastic about Marika's engagement ring, about their wedding plans, oohing delightedly at her responses to our requisite questions. But Lisa avoided my eyes.

"It wouldn't have gone anywhere anyway," I told her that evening. "Just like with me and Pentti."

She suspended her fork halfway to her mouth, her head turned quizzically to one side, a bemused smile signalling her irritation. "What are you talking about?"

I nodded to the table across the room where Yuri sat like a potentate among the four adoring women.

"Oh don't be silly." She frowned to be sure I knew I had intruded. "Besides, that Pentti was just trying to get you to bed."

My face went hot. Lisa and I did not talk like that, certainly not with each other. Sex was taboo, something we might talk about with our close friends, never within the family. We had long ago agreed to consider our bodies chalices to be reserved for the holy sacrament of marriage. It was our souls men were supposed to find irresistible. Besides, she was right. Pentti's proposal of marriage had probably been a ploy to get beyond my American puritanism. The night he showed up in my hotel room with a small bag packed with pajamas and toothbrush was the night I told him to get lost. Perhaps it was the combination. There was something calculated and unromantic about seducing a woman with your pajamas and toothbrush at hand.

But I had never told Lisa any of this. She only knew of his proposal and had been horrified that I was even considering it.

"What a thing to say!" I exploded in prudish horror.

She smiled sweetly. "Well, isn't it true? Isn't that why you're red as a beet?"

We finished our dinner without further talk. Lisa went to join some others playing cards. I returned to the dorm and spent the evening in bed with a book.

The next day we were invited on a ten kilometer ski with a group, including Marika and her friends. I had not skied much so was not in very good condition. But the tundra did not seem very demanding, the trail weaving among the fells rather than up and down them. Ten kilometers passed in no time what with the stops and camaraderie. But I was happy to arrive at last at the site where we would have the lunch provided by the lodge. Everyone flopped down in the sun as we passed sausages and cheese, bread and fruit, with a choice of beer or various sodas.

"Don't eat too much," a man warned Lisa and me. "It's always longer going back, and you don't want to be full." He was a man of indeterminate age who had tried several times since our arrival to make conversation with either one of us. His English was fluent, and he seemed nice enough, but talking for him was a struggle. It was as though he was surrounded by a jell of solitude that had taken years to accumulate and which he might only pierce out of necessity or desire. There was no necessity between us and desire, if it had ever existed, existed now as absence: in his body, his voice, and most of all, in his eyes.

"How long will we rest?"

"About two hours."

Two hours seemed a long time. I ate to my fill, and drank, though I avoided the beer. Lisa and I tried to converse with the others, including our gentleman friend. The others gradually slipped into Finnish or German; our friend ran out of talk. We lay back on the snow, groggy in the warm sun after the long ski. We even dozed.

Marika and a few others were up on their skis. They were excited, pointing to the top of a large fell that overlooked our picnic spot.

"Oh, let's go," Lisa cried.

We scrambled onto our skiis and followed the small group. Our friend warned us again. "We're going back soon, you know. You don't want to get too tired. It's a long way."

We laughed. I pointed upwards. "I can't miss that. It's the best part, you know. Coming down."

By the time Lisa and I were about two-thirds of the way, the others were coming down with whoops and cries of delight. We turned and joined them.

The rest of the group was packed and ready to go when we got down.

"It is easy to get lost in the tundra," Yuri had warned us on our first lesson. To demonstrate, he pointed with his ski pole in a large circle. Everywhere we looked was the same, no identifying features anywhere to guide us. "Never come here without a guide," he had said.

Perhaps one kilometer passed. I pushed myself to get up beside Lisa, just in front of me.

"I'm tired," I said, breathless. "Can we stop or something?"

"I don't think so," she said without pausing. "It'll get dark." I stopped to rest. The line pushed onward, Lisa with them.

I let the rest of the line pass. My legs felt like jelly. I believed if I could rest just a few minutes, I could regain my breath and strength. I sank down and looked off into the vastness all around me. I took a handful of snow.

"Don't eat snow!"

I was startled. It was our friend, again, the one with the warnings. He'd left the line and come back for me.

"I'm so thirsty."

I sipped at the snow on my mitten. No sooner had it melted on my tongue than I wanted more.

"No snow," he repeated. "It just makes it worse. I know the way, but we have to keep going. If it gets dark, I won't find the way back. Get up."

He took the lead position and established a slow rhythm. He made no attempt at conversation; we just concentrated on keeping going. The others had disappeared out of view.

He was an engineer, single, on vacation. He said he loved Lapland and skiing. He did not ask me about myself, just kept encouraging me to keep moving.

"It's over here," he said, "just over this fell. Not far now."

I was ready to give it up. To rest, to sleep, to let my body stop, was all I wanted, I didn't care what happened. Besides, he had already said that three times: just over this fell, and we had climbed and there was no sign of the lodge, just more fells to climb and go down. I felt hopeless.

He went to the top of this latest fell as I sank down once again.

"Here," he called, "here it really is!"

I could scarcely believe my eyes. The lodge was just below the ridge, so close I could smell the dinner being served. It was dusk. We had just made it.

I dragged myself down the hallway toward our room. Lisa met me in the hall, freshly changed, on her way to the dining room.

"Take a sauna," she said.

Marika's head poked out the dormitory door. "Oh, you're back. I'm so glad. We were worried. Yes, take a sauna, you'll see."

"I just want to sleep," I said. "I've never been so exhausted in my life."

"No, no, come here." Marika took my jacket off, my hat and mittens, then sat me down and pulled off my boots. She grabbed a towel. "Come on." She was laughing as she pulled me down the hall to the sauna room. "Now take off your own clothes or I'll call everyone to come and take them off for you!"

I protested, but she threatened to make good on her promise. "You'll see. You won't believe you are the same person after you take sauna. Now strip!"

"I feel great," Lisa said. "I wouldn't believe them, but it's true. You'll see. Then come and eat."

It was true. I sat almost an hour in the hot room, then took a cold shower. My muscles relaxed, I felt as though I had done nothing more strenuous than a mild workout. In the dining room, I ate ravenously. Lisa was sitting across the room with Marika and Yuri. A fire was burning hot in the large open fireplace, its light and shadows playing across their three faces. Lisa looked beautiful, her earnest, shy eyes looking now at Marika, now at Yuri. I couldn't hear their conversation, only the fire that cracked and spat filling the room with its wood odor. It was one of those silences, redolent with pine and warmth, the kind that touches in unexpected ways. I saw the engineer across the room, seated alone, his gaze unseeing out the window into the dark void. I would never know his name.

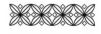

To love her means to be hurt by her. Even now, remembering is like lowering myself into a tub of very hot water. I sink in, prepared, as soon as my skin can tell me, to leap out with a mock yelp that turns serious at the very real burn.

Over the years, I have actually denied loving Lisa. I told myself, and others, that we were not really that close. I transformed my memories of her: she was an unhappy girl, moody, mostly grumpy; she made me feel guilty; she was perhaps even mentally ill at some point. All of the above may be true, but it is also only partially so. Until I sat down with this material, I never questioned this image of her, nor my motives for it. Until I sat down to write this, I did not hurt so consciously. Oh, I had wept, I had mourned, but I had mainly stayed angry. Anger allowed me to remain aloof. It protected me, I thought.

In the America of the Fifties and early Sixties, children were raised to "face reality"; imagination was a realm reserved for children and artists. For young women this "real" world could be summed up pretty much in the choice of a husband, the quest of our lives reduced to that. And though imagination might flourish regarding this subject, reality always interjected itself in the form of the boyfriend, the date, the prospect. Whatever he was, that was to be one's life. It was not always a pretty sight.

What I observed of the world called reality was far from the exciting world of make-believe and play I had inhabited throughout childhood. Outwardly, I took on the dull mantle expected of me; inwardly, I maintained a private life within a dreamy imagination. Far into my teens I remained the heroine of a film for hours after I'd left the theatre. I had her chin, the puzzled pucker between her brows, I was incredibly sensual, or wise, filled with worldly emotions, ambition, fateful love, whatever. On the way home in the back seat of the car, I'd watch the familiar scenery pass as if seeing it all for the first time, through these new eyes.

Travelling through Europe was like that, except I *was* the heroine travelling toward my destiny beneath the poignant whistle of a European train. Europe was real, I was its imagination. It was the perfect marriage.

Lisa and I quickly created a comfortable routine: mornings we had tea and bread together either in our room or a nearby cafe, then went our separate ways until lunchtime when we'd meet and tell each other of our adventures, what we'd seen or done, what had happened. Afternoons we usually chose to do something together, unless we couldn't agree, then again we separated to each do what she most wanted, to meet later at our hotel or pension in order to have dinner together. We never went anywhere alone at night. Not because we were fearful. Nights just lent themselves to loneliness, requiring a social life the days didn't.

With a budget limiting us to less than $5.00 a day, we nevertheless made dinner an occasion, dressing up, changing our tourist gum-soled shoes for a pair of heels, and having a bottle of cheap wine with whatever we ordered. Any restaurant was romantic and extraordinary in our eyes. We did not need the allure of first-class establishments; every place we entered became a first-class establishment. It shone in our eyes, lighting up under our admiration and enthusiasm, as did also the waiters whose quick assessment did not miss us as innocents abroad. We must have made a tacit agreement about men because, though we never discussed a policy, we also never picked anyone up, or allowed anyone to pick us up. We were American girls after all; we'd long ago understood the peril of being female and single.

Except in Venice. And why not? Venice is the place I would have chosen to dream into existence if I could ever have imagined it; for seven days and nights it was the reality Lisa and I awakened into like Sleeping Beautys within her enchanted spell.

Besides Venice was Italian. Italian meant home, or as close to home as we had been since leaving ten months before. Having grown up among Italian-Americans, we found the people familiar, the men unthreatening, despite their gift for creating auras of irresistible lust around themselves the moment a woman entered their view. Even with its fairy tale atmosphere, Venice contained a comforting humanity; it felt welcoming.

We arrived in the late afternoon by train, met by the ubiquitous hotel porters calling out their hotels' rates in three or four languages, pulling at our luggage, sure we could not resist such low prices. We followed one though the narrow streets to his family home where we stayed for the sum of one dollar each per night, including the European breakfast of tea with crusty rolls we were becoming addicted to. We had been travelling two weeks already, through Denmark and Germany, and, if anything, had gained in enthusiasm and a thrilled awareness of how lucky we were. We drank whatever was put in front of us, slept in whatever cheap hotel we found. Our only requirement was that the rooms be clean: no bed bugs, no roaches—or none that we could see.

Other than a trip to Murano, and the events I'm about to describe, I can scarcely recall anything specific that we did in Venice. I know this was the one place where Lisa and I did not separate. We shared all of it together, strolling the alleys, loitering on the bridges by the ancient walls that rose up out of the water, thick powerful walls quivering like water lilies in the water below. Everything was mirrored in Venice, giving one a double vision as the solidity of the world above dissolved on the surface of the water below. Venice revealed that vulnerability which gives our seemingly solid world its shimmering beauty. It is a mirage built upon the sea, reminding us of that other sea upon whose surface all our words and ideas, our very lives, flit like the wisps they are, into whose depths everything disappears.

We spent hours just looking at that play of light and shadow on the water. We listened to the lives of the Venetians in the small plazas or as their voices emerged from the deep-set windows, now longing, now wooing, now cajoling. The Italian language was not one either of us knew, but its music was familiar from what its immigrant sons and daughters had brought to our American tongue. Vowels that could be cradled like infants when spoken in love or sympathy, the consonants equally softened as though hushed for the sleeping child, suddenly became the shrieks of gulls, the calls of crows, thrust against consonants so sharp one might cut one's teeth on them. Anger was public, emotion boisterously apparent. We loved it; after so long in a northern world, summer had arrived for us, in ambience as well as in season.

And so when we met Tony in St. Mark's Square, we did not defend ourselves against his approach as we had all previous offers. Part of that might be explained by his garb that clearly identified him as a gondolier. To us, gondoliers were like knights from another time. They rode the canals, guiding the dark mysterious boats with a horseman's grace.

"American," he announced, meaning us, and nodded appreciatively at his acumen when we responded that yes we were.

"Gondolier," he went on, pointing to his chest. He settled next to me on the stone parapet. "Tony." He shook my hand, formally like a Northerner, then Lisa's. "You want ride?"

Lisa and I exchanged looks and laughed. We had taken the one gondola ride we could afford. Now we walked, or took the large bus boats.

"No," I said, "but thanks."

His face opened in amazement. "No? No? You no want gondola ride?"

Lisa was about to make up some explanation. She was good at that, and it annoyed me. I liked things plain, straight. I interrupted her smiling apology that I could see Tony was having trouble understanding anyway.

"No money," I said, my hands open to illustrate emptiness.

"Ah, *si.*" He laughed. "You no understand. See?" He pointed toward the Grand Canal. "*My* boat." Maybe fifty gondolas, some with drivers in them, were parked along the esplanade. "My boat," he again emphasized.

"He wants to give us a ride," I said quickly in a low voice to Lisa. She was irritated that I'd indicated we couldn't afford the ride. She looked off across the plaza.

"You," Tony said and pointed first at me, then to Lisa, "you my, how you say, my....?" He was frowning helplessly, his hand across his breast.

"Guests," I provided. "Like friends, you mean. You want to give us a free ride. Is that right?"

"Barbara!" Lisa breathed.

"I'm only clarifying," I responded. "We don't have to accept."

"Yes!" Tony cried. "Friends! We go picnic."

Now we were both puzzled. "Picnic?" Lisa was looking around. "Where?"

Tony pointed out toward the sea. "There," he said with a note of triumph. "Ocean picnic."

I liked his openness, his apparent innocence. I shrugged and looked at Lisa. She also shrugged. "So where do we get food?"

Tony became serious. "First you meet my friend."

Another young man, very different in dress and demeanor, had, unnoticed, joined the three of us, standing off to one side.

"Piero," Tony announced. "Lisa. Barbara," my name said with trilled r's. Piero ducked his head after each introduction. He kept his hands in his pockets. Where Tony was expansive, Piero was withdrawn, guarded. Not even his eyes revealed much, which

I thought odd for an Italian. He and Tony, Tony doing most of the talking, had a fairly long exchange in Italian, then Tony waved us along. "Come," he said. "We get food."

The burly gondolier led the way through the narrow streets occasionally booming out a popular Italian tune as we threaded our way among the many pedestrians. Lisa had fallen back a ways, as had Piero, so I ended up more or less with Tony as my escort. Wherever he went, he was greeted loudly with big slaps on the back, his hand pumped enthusiastically. Lisa and I were looked over with appreciation, not unlike the sausages Tony chose for us in one meat shop, or the long rolls of crusty bread he chose in another along with two kinds of cheese.

"Fruit," he cried. "We need fruit," and led us down another circuitous route to find his particular stand. He was carrying everything, his arms nearly full.

I said, "Piero, why don't you carry something?"

Tony mocked. "Piero don't carry things."

Piero laughed. Lisa and I offered to carry the bread and cheese.

"No, no, Tony do it. Tony is gondolier. Piero is student. He is rich."

"So why is the gondolier paying for everything then?" I whispered to Lisa. She hushed me, but Piero, who clearly heard, just laughed.

"I don't get it," I insisted to Tony as we walked ahead now on our way back to the square. "What does Piero's being rich mean that he can't carry a loaf of bread? Are you his servant or something?"

Tony's good humor momentarily evaporated. "I am not servant. I am gondolier." Apparently this was supposed to explain both men's behavior. It wasn't important, I dropped it, but vaguely disliked this Piero who carried nothing, not even a wallet apparently.

"Aristocrat," Tony said quietly with a nod back toward his friend.

I had already learned with utmost clarity in the months I had lived in Finland how quintessentially American I was. However askew might be the lessons of the mixed and not always melted society in which I lived, I had learned too deeply the one about equality, at the very least, its possibility. So the word *aristocrat* meant nothing in terms of social position. To me, aristocrat was a word reserved for particular character traits, and could occur in any human being regardless of the circumstances of class or birth or race. Tony seemed more of an aristocrat to me than this Piero slinking along halfheartedly in our wake.

With calls and curses and snatches of song, Tony maneuvered us through the traffic on the Grand Canal much as he had through the pedestrians in the narrow passages of the city. The occasional speedboat was what brought forth the curses as it left behind a plume of waves the flat-bottomed gondola was never designed to negotiate. The string of words that comprised the curse was about equal to the length of the passer's wake with as much froth and foam, and was ignored, the inhabitants of the passing boat oblivious to anything other than the putt-putt of their engine, the sign of their status and wealth. Tony was defender of the old Venice, the city of silence, of mirrored presence. These noisy boats not only threw his gondola into a dangerous pitch unless he turned it to take the waves head-on, they rattled among the old walls with the noise of progress, omen of loss and change.

"They destroy Venezia," he cried out, ostensibly to Lisa and me, but more to the world at large.

Piero sat in the bow with Lisa. Her patience revealed his shyness at an English much inferior to his compatriot Tony whose need to communicate overcame any reluctance he might have about making a fool of himself. Lisa spoke with her hands, her Spanish and limited French, mostly with the delicate femininity that she embodied the way others might possess beauty or intelligence. She was intelligent to be sure, and sometimes beautiful, depending on her moods which swung her back and forth between darkness and light, but these, along with all other traits, were subservient to a pervasive femininity that appeared as an elegance, a great delicacy.

She sat, back straight, knees together, hands wrapped around her knees, head leaned to one side as she listened with apparent interest to Piero's struggle to convey something which might or might not be dull or bright, one could never tell with Lisa.

Tony, pushing the long oar, was intent upon its rhythm and the swell of the waves. Finally, he stopped. The boat rocked as it drifted now without its rudder, the gondolier.

"I'm hungry," he announced. He produced the packages of cheese and bread and fruit and flopped down on the seat beside me. Lisa flashed me a look that told me she wanted out of here as soon as politely possible.

I, however, was still caught in the thrill of being taken on an ocean picnic in a gondola outside Venice. I was also balking, as I sometimes did, at the role I often had thrust upon me by others, Lisa among them, who had decided themselves too polite, too delicate, too sensitive, too whatever, to face a situation directly. This had happened many times between Lisa and me, the most recent a volatile situation that developed when an African man we met on our ski trip in northern Finland had become persistent in his pursuit of Lisa. After avoiding him for days as best she could, he cornered the two of us in the hallway outside our room.

"You don't like me because I'm a black man," he said with the whine of the self-righteous when Lisa refused to go to the bar with him, making up some face-saving excuse. "I know you Americans. That's the way you are. You don't like black people." He said this with triumph, as if he had discovered a great truth.

"You are a lucky man," I said levelly, making sure his eyes held mine. "How nice it must be to have an excuse like that to hide behind. In fact, my sister doesn't want to go out with you because you are obnoxious. But you don't need to acknowledge this, do you? You can pretend it's because you're black. Fine. But just leave her alone."

I was terrified. He, I think, was simply flabbergasted. To our relief, he avoided us for the rest of the time we were there. Months later, he married a girl from Rovaniemi; soon after, we heard he was wanted by Interpol. He apparently had married a woman in just about every European country he had visited.

Lisa had been grateful for my interference; she'd felt trapped, and was. But other times she took me to task for these same characteristics, calling me tactless or insensitive. So I'd come to resent having to get us out of situations where Lisa's more hidden devices were not going to work. I didn't know what might be going on between her and Piero. It was broad daylight; we were in a boat in the middle of a bay with gondolas, boats and boat busses passing within view; I figured whatever was going on was merely irritating, a minor inconvenience to her. And I liked Tony's company. He was jovial and generous. He reminded me of many of the boys and young men I'd grown up with. Besides, I was also hungry.

Tony and I broke up the bread; he cut the cheese into thick slices, and quartered the fruit. With my mouth full, I reached across to pass Lisa some bread. She was staring at me, that look of do-something-Barbara on her face. Then I saw. Piero's hand was behind Lisa, but I saw from the way her blouse was moving that he was fondling her.

Tony noticed too and half-laughed, then said something low and fast in Italian. Piero ignored him. His eyes were distant. I felt a confusion of irritation and disgust. What a pig he was. Whatever pleasure might be involved was clearly for himself alone. Lisa squirmed away, but he just moved closer. But why couldn't she just say something? Was she too much of a lady to tell him to cut it out? Her eyes were on mine.

"Piero!" I shouted. He jumped, his attention returned. "Leave her alone," I said more quietly. I hadn't planned on yelling, it just came out. Lisa was blushing.

"Hey," Tony said quietly. "Maybe we go back. Here," he handed Piero a sandwich and a peach, probably to keep both hands occupied. He nodded to Lisa. "You sit here."

Lisa moved quickly to the seat indicated with her back to Piero. She was hunched over, pulled into herself. Then her eyes and mine met, and we both thought of our first encounter with the notorious Italian pinch and burst out laughing as we had on that occasion as well. It wasn't the appropriate response then, nor was it now, but Tony at least was grateful, I could see that. He started singing loudly, his good humor returning as quickly as it had disappeared in his embarrassment.

Lisa and I doubled over with pain, we laughed so hard. We knew we should have known better. You just didn't allow yourself to get picked up like that. Even in Italy, even in Venice. We could never speak of it without bursting into tearful laughter. We never saw Tony or Piero again. But the word *aristocrat* always brought back that memory, always carried the double meaning—the true versus the hereditary, the real versus the imagined.

Mother would never figure it out. "I want you girls to marry someone high class," she often said.

"You mean like an aristocrat?" one of us would respond and then laugh hard for minutes. Mother would make a face. She knew there were things we'd never tell her. But this one never made sense.

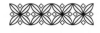

I did not attend Lisa's funeral, nor did I go to see her grave, next to my father's, in a cemetery in Baltimore.

At the time it seemed a matter of money. I had flown East to see my father before he died, knowing that I wouldn't be able to afford another trip for his funeral. That seemed all right. I hated funerals, and I preferred seeing him, however ill, as my living father than as a corpse.

That now seems to me an intellectualized position. Forget the lack of money for the moment because I probably would have made the same choice even if money had been available. And I believe such a choice is a mistake. Yes, I should have gone to see my father alive, but I should also have gone to his and Lisa's funerals. It is important to take leave of a father, a sister. The fact that I lived three thousand miles away and saw them seldom during the years since I'd left home took away the immediacy of their loss. Their deaths were something I could only feel through language.

"Dad's dead," I told myself. "Lisa killed herself." Words were the source of my knowledge and of my experience.

She looked so small, someone told me after her funeral. More words. I wasn't there, I didn't even send flowers. Nothing.

Only once did I momentarily consider taking my life. I was around seventeen, and filled with a worldly sorrow that I enhanced by lying around listening to mournful jazz. I actually walked into the bathroom and, watching my face in the mirror, took out my Dad's razor blades. Imaginatively I cut my wrists and watched the blood flowing against the white sink. That was it; that was as close to death as I ever wanted to get. To choose death was unfathomable. By not going to Lisa's funeral, in some peculiar way, I was refusing to accept that it happened. I would not see it, or have it touch me directly.

I live in a small Hispanic village now where death is acknowledged, is part of the lives of everyone. It is not loved, or desired, but when it occurs, the whole village turns out to murmur greetings to the family, and to take a final look at the one who's gone. Everyone stands at the gravesite, after the services, whether Protestant or Catholic, and waits until the coffin is lowered into the open hole. It is done then, and there is no doubt in anyone's mind that one of us has died and now lies in the earth beneath garlands of bright plastic flowers that rattle in the high mountain winds.

In Spring, rainbows collected in neon hues at the edges of the oil-slick mud puddles. You had only to position yourself just right to focus on the technicolor surface, rich and elegant in contrast to the dark, soggy ground. No amount of stirring or stomping dispersed their forms; they simply reshaped themselves, sliding back to the puddles' edges. More than the robin, or forsythia, the oil-slick puddles of melted snow presaged the coming warmth. Theirs was the first return of color to the earth.

I was reminded of the puddles as I watched the landscape below. The sun was just lightening the eastern sky toward which the plane travelled, and the tiny lakes below lit up like glow-worms. Either they were covered with oil slick, like those puddles, or the angle of the light hit them like a prism because, as the plane travelled above them, momentary rainbows flitted across their surfaces.

Scattered around the lakes were houses, most of them dark, but a few with lights on, the light spilling out the windows like the aura around a body. I mused about the lives inside, as I had always done about lives led in other houses, with the familiar regret that I could not live them all. It was limiting to be one person with only one life.

The dawn light gathered strength on the horizon; below me, the light from others' kitchens cast shadows on the patches of leftover snow. Three hours before, the Los Angeles night had been lit by a full moon which, as the plane headed briefly west on its take-off, travelled both above the plane where it belonged in the sky, and below it on the ruffled water of the Pacific. Each of these kinds of light had its own character and mood; I toyed with finding words to catch their individual essences. I believed in words; believed that language could capture things in their reality. It was not enough that these lights should just be, that I should respond to each differently, I wanted to identify them. To be able to express their essences in words filled me with such an indescribable joy that that was enough for me to fail to notice how I ceased to experience the light itself.

I noticed it now, however, and remembered how in Germany with Lisa some years before, we had laughed together at our fellow American tourists who, so busy taking pictures of castles and vineyards along the Rhine, missed seeing the objects of their photographs. Between camera sightings, they drank beer and talked about home or the difficulties of travelling among 'foreigners'.

"Oh, there's a good one. Hurry up, Harry, before we pass."

Harry would leap up adjusting the camera, snap, take one quick look—"Ah yes, pretty"—and reseat himself with a large sip of the good German beer.

"They'll never see Germany until they get their film developed," Lisa whispered. Lisa and I, of course, looked intently at everything. So intently in fact that by the time we got into New York harbor, we were so church-, castle-, and museum-logged that I would sleep through the Statue of Liberty though I had longed to experience the immigrant's view of America, and Lisa would sigh deeply as we stood on the deck overlooking the city.

"For a moment," she half-laughed, "I was bracing myself for yet another stint of heavy-duty sightseeing. How refreshing to be home, to be no longer obligated to take in all that culture."

Lisa and I had spent altogether one year in Europe—nine months in northern Finland teaching English, and three months travelling. For both of us, though we had lived all our lives in the same small house, though we were sisters, that year was the first time we had gotten to know one another. Lisa would be in

Baltimore where I was now headed, had in fact just moved to Georgetown in order to start her new government job.

"The CIA!" my father had shouted.

"Well, what is that anyway?" I asked.

"Don't you even know the composition of your own government? What did I send you kids to college for?" His voice over the three thousand miles of telephone lines expressed his disgust. "The Central Intelligence Agency. Do you know what that is?"

"Dad," I had laughed with a mixture of embarrassment and hauteur. "You know I don't know about those kinds of things. They don't interest me."

There was a pause in which I sensed he was struggling to control his parental need to inform and educate, having learned, having in fact himself said, that children learned through experience, not through lectures and, in spite of that knowlege, had spent his four children's teen years futilely lecturing.

"It's a spy agency. My own daughter a spy!"

"A spy?" I could not understand what that had to do with intelligence, a trait I regarded highly. "You mean Lisa's going to be a spy?" I could not believe this, and laughed. "Dad, that's just too wild. I mean, wild."

"It's not funny."

"I can't believe it. They must do other things besides spy, don't you think?"

"No. She's part of that whole McCarthy-like mentality. It makes me sick."

McCarthy. I vaguely recalled hearings on the tv during high school, but thought better than to ask him what all that was.

"Talk to her, please." My father had never pleaded with me. I was struck by the tone in his voice. "See if you can talk her out of it. Wait a minute." The phone went hollow until I heard my mother's voice.

"Hi."

"Hi, Mom. What's this all about?"

"Listen. Just leave her be. Your Dad and I don't agree on this. I don't like her working for that place any more than he does, but it's a good job with good money and she needs something like that. She was going crazy here, you know that."

I shrugged. "Don't worry. Lisa wouldn't listen to me anyway."

And so I had said nothing and heard nothing further. Lisa had had to finish out a teaching contract so had not begun her training until these last few weeks. And news of what was happening in her life got lost in the family's preoccupation with Dad's sudden illness.

"We don't know what it is, but he's very weak and vomits a lot," Mother had said. That was January.

"He's getting cobalt treatments. He can hardly stand up now. Yes, it's cancer." February.

March. Hesitation. Finally, "The doctor doesn't think he's going to make it. No, of course he doesn't know. Because it's too horrible, that's why."

And so this last week into March I was on my way to see him.

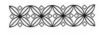

When I was visiting my parents for that week while my father was dying, Lisa asked me to go back with her to see her new apartment. I couldn't. It didn't feel right. I was there for my parents, not for her. I had no idea there was something for her I should be there for, though I saw the disappointment in her eyes, and I did want to see the town, particularly her place. I would have enjoyed it. That was the trouble. I believed it would be callous to enjoy anything. Perhaps Lisa needed to talk. But she never let on. She just clearly and insistently let me know she wanted me to come, and even that wasn't unusual.

I begged off. I don't blame myself for that. I was too young to know that joy and pain are not strangers, that, in the midst of sorrow, one can laugh. And maybe she didn't need to talk. Maybe she really did just want to show me her new life, to give me a little pleasure while I was there. She had been at my parents' side throughout the ordeal of my father's illness. She was more accustomed to it than I. So perhaps she just wanted to do me a favor. I have never believed she killed herself just because she was pregnant. She had talked about suicide for more than a year already. Pregnancy for a Catholic young woman in 1966 was a serious matter. But not one of life and death. Far worse no doubt was the rejection she received from the man. But even that is not enough.

Lisa was something of a trail-blazer, at least within the world of our family. She pushed beyond all the limits that I, at least, accepted as part of what I might have termed "the real world". She travelled, got fabulous jobs. She dreamed, and found ways to fulfill the impossible. She was a creator. She knew how to manipulate reality to achieve her goals. Just having goals was an anomaly for a woman of her generation and background. So perhaps what happened was that the impossible, with all of its challenges, was grinding down to the merely possible. Life was no longer an endless series of doors yet to be opened. There were only a few and, for a woman of talent and ambition, that must have been a devastating understanding. And now, pregnant, abandoned by the man she believed she loved, the future was no longer a movement toward possible dreams. Everything was entirely, and too sleazily, possible.

That she was training for work in the CIA could not have helped. What the CIA had to teach her, from the little she told me with a certain cynical amusement, was duplicity, deceit, delusion, all of this in direct contradiction to the values with which she had been raised; indeed, as my father, a decent, lifelong conservative, argued, in direct opposition to the values of a democracy itself. That she had to play-act as part of her job training, practice lying as a professional skill, could not have helped a woman already looking with longing down the long dark corridor of death.

But I'm doing it. I'm giving reasons. I'm explaining. When she first discussed suicide with me eight months before, none of these conditions existed. Yet even then she intended it. She meant it. And then, given more excuses than anyone ever needed, did it.

His hands were mine. Because he was so thin. Because his hands lay on his chest on top of the turned-down sheet and I was standing there having just greeted him. The fingers were long and delicate, the man's muscles gone. What was left were my hands, the woman coming out in him.

He was surprised to see me. "Barbara! What are you doing here?"

I lied.

"And where's your family?"

I lied again. I wouldn't look at my mother and sister-in-law. I hated lying like this. I looked at him. He was definitely my father. The smile, the way his lips thinned out and the corners turned up, a big long smile, the whole face opening with it, as if the lower half of his face were a wide skirt and invisible hands lifted the edges and the whole face curtsied. His eyes were tired. There wasn't that sharpness, the sudden anger or compassion or just the faraway dream they used to take him to mornings when he'd sit over four, five cups of coffee looking out the window at the tops of the trees. He'd cross his legs always, seldom sat without at least his ankles crossed. Never with his legs wide the way men most often do. And his body. You could see in the way the covers fell sharply down with sudden shadows the ribs, the drop at their base where the belly begins, legs like slats, hip bones like hatchets. And the hands.

I was grateful. I had expected a monster. I had expected a being unrecognizable but using my name, calling me his, and I would have to call him mine. I tried not to cry. I hated this pretense that he was not dying.

My mother had moved to Baltimore to be near Tommy and his wife. She had this small apartment with the remains of our family home scattered here and there. The whole place smelled of Lysol. He lay in the bedroom in one of the single beds. Boxes of giant diapers were piled in the hall. She was exhausted. She had been taking care of him for months.

We were sitting around the dinette table at the end of the kitchen. Mother asked me again to promise not to mention it. I began to argue, tried to point out how I would approach it, just leave a door open. I saw her fear. My sister-in-law looked over at me. "She promised," she told my mother. "Okay," I said, and dropped it.

Lisa came later and we went in together to sit with him. Lisa talked easily, too quickly, I thought, too much cheer. She was always the quiet one, the one with all of her kept secret within. Now she talked. About castanets, about her job. Her apartment. Talked. One time he looked at me and said, "I wonder what kind of disease this is." For one breath we stood together at this door. I turned away. Lisa said something about how he'd be up and around in no time, and jokingly, how he'd even be chasing women.

He looked down the length of his body. "No, not any-more. It's no good."

I must have looked surprised.

"Too much cobalt," he said.

He had never referred to the male sexual organ at all, let alone his own. He had never spoken of sex. I had never seen him be even slightly sensual toward my mother. Now he was pointing out his own penis to his two daughters. Perhaps because it was neuter. Too much cobalt. Cobalt. Cancer. He was filled with it. His penis was not the only part of him that had been neutered.

And he knew it. He had to know it. And I knew he knew it, knew also why I had come, why his third and oldest daughter would come later that day, both of us three thousand miles without our husbands and kids and with no holiday for an excuse. It was why I hated the lie. He'd studied pharmacy, knew medicine, what cobalt was for, why he couldn't eat, why his body was melting away. And one day, when I was alone with him and he called to me to bring the bedpan and I did and he peed a thickish red-brown blood, and the way he craned his head up off the pillow, his eyes opened wide to see down the length of his body to the dark blood, how he looked hard, made sure of what he saw, knew it was hopeless, but didn't say anything. Then when he saw that I saw, said it must be diarrhea and he knew I knew he lied. So nobody was fooled.

We didn't get another chance to talk. After that first day, he lay against the pillows, his lips moving, his eyes far beyond us, his hands and arms eloquent in pantomime.

"Boy!" he cried out over and over, the boy who was his guide delivering death like a newspaper smack against the door. But not his. Not yet. The boy kept passing and my father called out to him over and over.

Someone had to sleep in the room with him. He had fallen out of the bed once in the middle of the night. Mother was alone with him and, terrified, she called the custodian. He was so light, the man scooped him up like a child, she said, placed him back on the bed, tucked him in. I didn't sleep that night. His arms waved in the dimness that came in from the night light in the bathroom and sometimes he would sit up and I would push him down so he wouldn't fall. And "Boy! Boy!" all night. I wanted him to die. I wanted to open the windows, let in the cold night air so the cough would smother him. I believed if we had all faced it together, he wouldn't need this stranger child to help him die. It was his kindness that he didn't tell us. Our fear which he must have seen, the pretense we made of everything being all right. We die alone. Or with a young boy bicycling precariously toward us from the distance.

My father was strong. And stubborn. He wanted to live. It was several weeks more after Ellie and I had left that Mother awakened one morning with his absence there in the room with her.

Ten years later I dreamed of him. His hair fell in long white strands, his body was full again, and he had his smile, though it was clear he was dead in this life. I asked for his blessing on my life, and he gave it. We embraced then and I told him it was all right, he could go, I was a woman now. I didn't need him as a father anymore. But he hasn't gone. Perhaps he didn't believe me. He never thought of me as more than a child. It's all right. I like having him around.

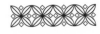

Not quite a year before Lisa died, all of us came back home for a reunion. Tommy, Ellie and I arrived with our spouses and children. Lisa was there. She had been living at home for several months now.

Sometime during the hectic and happy days, I had about an hour alone with Lisa. She lay on her stomach on the sofa, I sat on the floor. She seemed so much more available to me than she ever had before, and talked with nostalgia of the happy years she'd recently spent working in Panama. She'd met a man there, one she said she loved, but other things she said made it clear to me that already there were serious problems, the main one being his reluctance to get seriously involved with her. It was also clear she wanted to ignore that reality. Dreamily, she spoke of him and how someday they'd probably marry, though she didn't see how she could bear to live in the Midwest where he was now settled and apparently wanted to stay.

We also reminisced about our year together in Finland and Europe, laughed at incidents and details, particularly about our feeble efforts to learn the castanets when in Spain. To my astonishment, she pulled out a pair of them and played the intricate rhythms with amazing dexterity. She, always the self-conscious and awkward one, got up and showed me some of the Latin dances she now did with a dancer's grace and fluidity. I was again amazed. She spoke with affection for the Panamanian people among whom she'd chosen to live rather than in the 'zone' where the vast majority of North Americans resided, and with bitterness toward the government that forced her to leave when there was trouble between Panama and the U.S. She had taught English for the U.S. Information Agency for about five years, and loved her job. It was the Panamanian people who had taught her to be free enough to love herself in order to dance and express her inner rhythms. She felt lost now back in the States among these cool Northerners. The government would not allow any employees who had worked during the 'uprising' to return.

Somewhere in that hour, she spoke of suicide, of wanting to die. I, the baby sister, then in my mid-twenties, married, with a child and all the responsibilities, and presumed wisdom, that maturity is supposed to bring, considered her words. I did not truly believe she was serious, but I wanted to jar her into awareness of such a possibility, wanted her to see how horrible it was. I must have believed her enough to have wanted to awaken her. And so I told her to be sure she did it right; otherwise she could end up a vegetable, or severely handicapped.

I understand today the utter foolishness of those words. I also understand I intended the words to have a reverse effect, but I can never quite forgive myself for having said them. I know now that with suicide there can be no tricks. To this day I wish I had said, "Please don't. I would miss you terribly." That might not have saved her in any case, but that would have been the truth.

"This won't hurt," he says.

I have heard that before.

But it doesn't. To my amazement, it doesn't. Two weeks later he says, "I can't get it. I'll have to cut the gum."

Initially, I had disliked him—young, red hair, cocky: "This won't hurt." And when it didn't, I had grown to like him; more and more each time I sat in the chair, I smiled at him genuinely, liking him. "He does know what he's doing," I thought. He became sure, confident, instead of cocky. But he can't fool me now. You don't cut a gum and tell your patient it won't hurt.

"Will it hurt?"

His eyes cloud. "Some people say it doesn't hurt at all."

I know the type.

"Will I be knocked out?"

"Of course not. I'll use a local."

The next day my whole jaw is swollen; even ice doesn't bring it down. I feel as though someone has socked me hard in the jaw:

Some neighbor kids and I ran down the fresh cut the water company men had made laying the new sewer pipe in the woods behind the house. The boys suddenly cut to the right toward the chicken coops. About to be ditched, I charged up the short slope, leaped, as they had, when I saw the one rusty strand of barbed wire. The other I didn't see because it was buried beneath the undergrowth. It sprang up, caught me behind the knee in the left leg. My body paused as though to gather in something. A shock. Like falling through ice. Like nothing that had ever happened before. I screamed from my belly where I felt the knee now, my whole body a single nerve into which the end of rusty barbed wire sank.

Dad came running. He was always my dubious savior, bringing more pain to release me from the current one, as now he leans down, his face twisted oddly, his voice calm, "This will hurt", and it does, it hurts more to tear it out, as he must. For a moment, I wish myself rooted like the nearby apple tree, preferring that to the release which shreds the nerve I am.

When it's out they take me to the neighborhood doctor. He had curly hair, glasses; his eyes were blue and kind, his shoulders straighter than my father's, somehow reassuring. He looked right at me, his eyes on mine and said, "This will hurt." He inserted the needle, all the time holding my eyes. I was transfixed. I felt it, but just couldn't let go the way I had earlier, somehow allowing pain to move out of me in the fibers of a scream because he looks at me with such sincerity—no flinching, no worry—and his eyes change then into something close to respect. "What a brave girl you are." I am surprised. My eyes are still swollen and red with the tears of before.

"That you didn't cry. You're very brave."

I swell with a wave of relief.

"Let me see if you can do that again."

The wave stops. I would, of course, try. It hurt, that second needle, and I bit my lip. But the wave swelled again when he said, "I can't believe this. You are so brave."

He walked toward the door. I felt good. "Let me call my wife. I want her to see this. She won't believe you're so brave." (They gave three tetanus shots in those days. I find this out much later.) I was close to tears. My bottom hurt almost as much as my knee. But I couldn't cry. Not now. She came in, and he let me have it again. They didn't even fuss much then, just a pat on the head, and him saying, "What a brave girl." I felt used somehow, torn as I was between my pride that I had not cried though I was so close to it and my feeling of betrayal, that he had merely tricked me.

How was I to know twenty years later I'd receive the words in scratchy type on the pale yellow paper: *Lisa is dead*? That the future is buried, a seed inside this peach moment of now. Each decision, each turning, contains its own partial birth of something else forming, until gradually, a pattern increases the embryo of tomorrow, so that you, Lisa, breathe into a phone for the last time, already gone too far beyond your voice.

It all rises out of this pain in my jaw.

"Can I follow you around?" Lisa asks me.

"Why?"

"I want to be thin like you," she says.

I notice for the first time her roundness, so unlike my body which is all angles. She wants to be like me, the youngest, the baby, as they call me. She wants to be skinny—"You look like an orphan," Mother says—like me. But she does not follow me around, has only said it. So she loses esteem in my eyes. She is fat now, and does not act upon her desires. She is strange, different, this is when I first notice it. She is maybe twelve, which would make me nine.

It would be dishonest if I claimed to remember the anniversary of Lisa's death every year. But I did for years. Perhaps one sign of healing is when the date arrives and, this time, you don't notice. May the 13th was a wounded day for me. I would think of Lisa many times during that day, with all of my regrets, sorrow, and blame.

The word 'grief' encompasses a wide range of feelings. It's a wonderful word, powerful, one whose sound so nearly expresses the state itself, with its clenched jaw and tight lamenting vowel that ends in the helpless final 'f'. Grief, as experienced, must pass through those various stages: rejection, lamentation, surrender.

Perhaps my grief is just ending. I hated Lisa's death. I refused it, railed at it; I also lamented, wept, and sorrowed; but I never surrendered to it. And so it did not end. I maintained my denial and sorrow through all these years.

In a poem I wrote some years ago on the anniversary of her death, I imagined that Lisa had returned on this, her day, and that I allowed her to use my body, to look out at the world through my eyes, to see what she had left behind. It was a misty, quiet day, the trees still bare against the early spring landscape (this was in Minnesota), and suddenly a church bell began to ring. I wrote:

Is it really you?
Or only the Sunday bell that rolls in like a foghorn?
I could almost believe we were at home again
the smell of the sea coming in like that.

That bell could tear your heart out.
Go ahead. Use mine.
Let it be torn.

I ended with an admonishment that I didn't want to hear her reasons for killing herself, and said with a satisfying cruelty that it was a pity she would have to miss again the just-opening lilacs.

The poem captures my state at the time totally, and my entrapment in those first two stages of grief for all these many years. I accept that. Without regret. Next spring, maybe the 13th of May, maybe not, I plan to visit Lisa's grave, at last to place on it the flowers of my love.

EPILOGUE

In late 1992 I went to Baltimore with my present husband and visited Dad's and Lisa's graves, which I was able to locate with the help of a reporter, Ann LoLordo, who chanced into my life at exactly the moment I needed her. Mother had died in 1986; Tommy had misplaced the information; Ellie didn't know. Ann found my expectation to locate the information in the Baltimore Hall of Records a little naive; even with her know-how, it took her months to find them.

When my husband and I first entered the cemetery what I felt most acutely was my own absence twenty-six years earlier. That I wasn't present then I felt with such regret that I imagined them all around me now: Mother and Tom, along with aunts, cousins, in-laws, entering in the slow-moving cars, their eyes darkened with sorrow, and at Lisa's funeral, with incomprehension, shock, stupor. This time I was with them to share the loss and sorrow.

As we left the cemetery, my first thought was that now it was over, something was completed. Even as the thought formed I realized nothing was over, nothing completed. Completion is just an idea we have about closing things: doors, books, lives. Closure. The word sounds so promising, so *final*. But after seeing their graves there, side by side, Dad's a bit wild with bunches of the crab grass he so hated in his own lawn, Lisa's demure, almost dainty, like the Lanz dresses she had loved to wear to accentuate her femininity, I realized this was just another part of my life with them. Closure is not about completion or endings; it is about a miraculous inner shift. Because what I saw as I stood above their graves, was that, at last, I was able to simply look, to take in what was in front of me without distortion from all my dark stories. Something had moved and the movement was in me. I lay down my bags of bitterness and guilt.

About the Author

Barbara McCauley was born, raised, and educated in Connecticut where she received her B.A. in English from Albertus Magnus College in New Haven. She taught English as a Second Language (ESL) to adult immigrants for fourteen years in Los Angeles, and was the principal writer of the bilingual Emmy Award winning television series *Pochtlán*.

She has also published two prior books of fiction, a book of her poetry, and three non-fiction titles on health related issues. In early 1992, McCauley returned to her lifelong passion of drawing from the figure and painting. Her work has been exhibited in both group and one-woman shows. She now lives in Truchas, NM where she and her husband, Alvaro Cardona-Hine, operate their own gallery and otherwise spend their time writing, painting, and watching clouds, ravens, and magpies.

※※※※

About the Press

Sherman Asher Publishing, an independent press established in 1994, is dedicated to changing the world one book at a time. We are committed to the power of truth and the craft of language expressed by publishing fine poetry, memoir, books on writing, and other books we love. You can play a role. Attend readings, teach classes, work for literacy, support your local bookstore, and buy poetry and literature.